"*Whiter Than Snow* is music for the sinner's soul. In fifty-two personal, creative, and sometimes poetic devotionals, Paul Tripp responds to Psalm 51 the way a jazz musician improvises on a familiar tune. In making this sweet music, Dr. Tripp makes King David's confession our own, helping us get honest about our sin and opening our hearts to the mercy of Jesus."
—PHILIP GRAHAM RYKEN, Senior Minister,
Tenth Presbyterian Church

"*Whiter Than Snow* is convicting and encouraging, cutting and healing. Paul Tripp delves into the misery of sin and the goodness of grace with insight and inspiration. This book wonderfully blessed me, and I pray for its widest possible reading."
—DANIEL L. AKIN, President; Professor of Preaching and Theology,
Southeastern Baptist Theological Seminary

whiter than snow

whiter than snow

meditations on sin and mercy

....

PAUL DAVID TRIPP

CROSSWAY BOOKS
WHEATON, ILLINOIS

Whiter Than Snow: Meditations on Sin and Mercy

Copyright © 2008 by Paul David Tripp

Published by Crossway Books
    a publishing ministry of Good News Publishers
    1300 Crescent Street
    Wheaton, Illinois 60187

Cover design: Jessica Dennis

Cover photo: Ilona Wellmann, Trevillion Images

First printing 2008

Printed in the United States of America

Unless otherwise indicated, Scripture quotations are from *The Holy Bible, English Standard Version*®, copyright © 2001 by Crossway Bibles, a publishing ministry of Good News Publishers. Used by permission. All rights reserved.

Scripture quotations marked MESSAGE are from The Message. Copyright © by Eugene H. Peterson 1993, 1994, 1995, 1996, 2000, 2001, 2002. Used by permission of NavPress Publishing Group.

Scripture references marked NIV are from *The Holy Bible: New International Version*®. Copyright © 1973, 1978, 1984 by International Bible Society. Used by permission of Zondervan Publishing House. All rights reserved.

The "NIV" and "New International Version" trademarks are registered in the United States Patent and Trademark Office by International Bible Society. Use of either trademark requires the permission of International Bible Society.

Scripture quotations marked AT are the author's translation.

PDF ISBN: 978-1-4335-0460-0

Mobipocket ISBN: 978-1-4335-0461-7

Library of Congress Cataloging-in-Publication Data
Tripp, Paul David, 1950–
    Whiter than snow : meditations on sin and mercy / Paul David Tripp.
      p. cm.
    ISBN 978-1-4335-0230-9 (tpb)
    1. Miserere—Meditations. I. Title.
BS1430.54.T75   2008
242'.5—dc22   2008004192

VP   18   17   16   15   14   13   12   11   10
15   14   13   12   11   10   9   8   7   6   5   4

I have lived it
and I know that it is true—
Your mercies are new every morning.

Contents

··

Preface
Once a Week with Mercy

It all started with a sleepless night, a condition that many of us can relate to. But it explodes into a story of lust, adultery, pregnancy, deception, and murder. If the story of David and Bathsheba were a television drama, you wouldn't watch it, or a paperback, you wouldn't choose to buy it. Yet, the terrible details of this ugly story splash across the pages of that religious book you and I call the Bible. Why would God preserve such a dark story? Who is the sex and blood of this story going to help anyway?

These are good questions to ask and worthy of answers. First, the New Testament (1 Corinthians 10) tells us that these things were written for our example and our instruction so that we would not fall into the same errors as God's people of old. Yes, this story is in the Bible because it is meant to be instructive. The details are not there to titillate you, but to help you understand things you need to understand about yourself, God, life in a fallen world, the nature of sin, and the power of God's transforming grace. Second, the Bible tells us that the people in this story were people just like us. As you read through the Bible, you know that its history is not filled with accounts of noble people who always did the right thing. No, the characters of the Bible, even the ones that we would tend to think of as heroes, were broken and flawed people. They, like us, were all sinners and, like us, all needed to be rescued by God's grace. "Rescued from what?" you might ask. Just like us, they needed to be rescued from themselves.

Think about David, whose story of temptation and sin is the backdrop of the psalm that provides the content for these meditations. When you read about all the war between nations and bloody power struggles that surrounded David's reign, it would be tempting to think that David's biggest enemy was the warring nation around him. But what this story demonstrates is that David carried his most powerful enemy around with him. That enemy lived inside of him. That enemy lives inside us as well. That enemy is called sin.

It would also be tempting to think that the greatest victory in David's life was his victory over the Philistines with their mighty Goliath. Yet this story, and the psalm that goes with it, points us to the fact that the greatest victory in David's life was not a victory of war but a victory of grace. It is amazing to watch this hardened adulterer and murderer brought to confession and repentance by the power of God's grace. And it is incredible that he does not lose his throne and, in fact, becomes a man who is known as "a man after God's own heart"! The greatest victory in David's life was not a victory of David's at all, but, rather, God's victory of grace over the sin that had captivated David's heart.

You'll never get David's story or the expansive helpfulness of Psalm 51 if you stand apart from the story and say to yourself, "I am so glad that I am not like David!" To say that completely misses the point. This story is in the Bible precisely because David's story *is* your story. No, I don't mean that you are an adulterer and a murderer. What I mean is that, like David, you are a sinner. There are times when you let yourself be ruled by your self-focused desires rather than by God's clear commands. There are times when you love something in the creation more than you love the Creator. There are times when you willingly step over God's boundaries in pursuit of what you want. There are times when your little kingdom of one means more to you than his transcendent kingdom of glory. There are times when you work hard to deny what you have done or to cover your tracks in fear of being caught.

David's story is our story, so Psalm 51 is our psalm as well. This psalm of moral failure, personal awareness, grief, confession, repentance, commitment, and hope wraps its arms around the experience of each one of us. These themes are in each of our lives. But the dominant theme of Psalm 51 is not sin. The dominant theme of Psalm 51 is grace. There would be no Psalm 51 if a God of boundless love hadn't sent Nathan to David as an instrument of rescuing mercy and restoring grace.

Psalm 51 is about how God meets us in our moments of deepest failure and transforms us by his grace. It is about how broken sinners can be brutally honest with God and yet stand before him without fear. All of the themes of sin, grace, and redemption are compacted into this powerful little psalm.

Come and look at yourself in the mirror of Psalm 51. Stop and look at the picture of your Lord that is painted by the words of this psalm. Let your ears hear the music of grace that is so beautifully played here. Take just one day a week and let yourself be transformed by the mercy that is not only the hope of this psalm but of your life and mine as well. And take time each week to celebrate the grace that is the greatest victory in your life as well.

Permit me to introduce the tool that you have in your hands. This is not the classic devotional that you are probably used to. Generally, those devotionals do a careful exegesis of a passage of the Bible and then draw out personal applications for you. This set of biblical meditations was put together in a very different way. Let me use a musical illustration. I have approached Psalm 51 like a piece of sheet music. The key signature, the time signature, the notes, and the dynamic markings that are on the page are there because that is precisely what the Great Composer designed to be there. This devotional book is not my attempt to help you to understand each note on the page. No, this book is more like jazz. While endeavoring to stay inside God's key signature and time signature, I have attempted to introduce to you creative, practical, everyday-life riffs on the themes that make up the music of grace of this wonderful psalm.

Think about it. This is exactly how you live your life as a Christian. God hasn't given you in the Bible the exact notes to play in every situation of your life. No, in the Bible, he gives you a divinely inspired musical structure (the history, command, principles, and perspectives that flow out of the narrative of Scripture) and invites you to improvise harmoniously with him. In this way, the life of a believer is more like jazz than it is like playing off sheet music. So, what you have in your hands is devotional jazz, designed to help you improvise more harmoniously with the Great Composer.

Because this psalm speaks into a dark moment of a child of God in the middle of the difficulties and temptations of life in a fallen world, it is brimming with themes that touch all of our lives. But the thing that is most engaging and exciting about this psalm is that no psalm plays the notes of God's grace better. The music of grace is meant to score the life of every believer. May it be so for you, and may this book contribute to making sweet improvisational music with your Redeemer right where you live every day.

The Story

....

The Story of David and Bathsheba

In the spring of the year, the time when kings go out to battle, David sent Joab, and his servants with him, and all Israel. And they ravaged the Ammonites and besieged Rabbah. But David remained at Jerusalem.

It happened, late one afternoon, when David arose from his couch and was walking on the roof of the king's house, that he saw from the roof a woman bathing; and the woman was very beautiful. And David sent and inquired about the woman. And one said, "Is not this Bathsheba, the daughter of Eliam, the wife of Uriah the Hittite?" So David sent messengers and took her, and she came to him, and he lay with her. (Now she had been purifying herself from her uncleanness.) Then she returned to her house. And the woman conceived, and she sent and told David, "I am pregnant."

So David sent word to Joab, "Send me Uriah the Hittite." And Joab sent Uriah to David. When Uriah came to him, David asked how Joab was doing and how the people were doing and how the war was going. Then David said to Uriah, "Go down to your house and wash your feet." And Uriah went out of the king's house, and there followed him a present from the king. But Uriah slept at the door of the king's house with all the servants of his lord, and did not go down to his house. When they told David, "Uriah did not go down to his house," David said to Uriah, "Have you not come from a journey? Why did you not go down to your house?" Uriah said to David, "The ark and Israel and Judah dwell in booths, and my lord Joab and the servants of my lord are camping in the open field. Shall I then go to my house, to eat and to drink and to lie with my wife? As you live, and as your soul lives, I will not do this thing." Then David said to Uriah, "Remain here today also, and tomorrow I will send you back." So Uriah remained in Jerusalem that day and the next. And David invited him, and he ate in his presence and drank, so that he made him drunk. And in the evening he went out to lie on his couch with the servants of his lord, but he did not go down to his house.

In the morning David wrote a letter to Joab and sent it by the hand of Uriah. In the letter he wrote, "Set Uriah in the forefront of the hardest fighting, and then draw back from him, that he may be struck down, and die." And as Joab was besieging the city, he assigned Uriah to the place where he knew there were valiant men. And the men of the city came out and fought with Joab, and some of the servants of David among the people fell. Uriah the Hittite also died. Then Joab sent and told David all the news about the fighting. And he instructed the messenger, "When you have finished telling all the news about the fighting to the king, then, if the king's anger rises, and if he says to you, 'Why did you go so near the city to fight? Did you not know that they would shoot from the wall? Who killed Abimelech the son of Jerubbesheth? Did not a woman cast an upper millstone on him from the wall, so that he died at Thebez? Why did you go so near the wall?' then you shall say, 'Your servant Uriah the Hittite is dead also.'"

So the messenger went and came and told David all that Joab had sent him to tell. The messenger said to David, "The men gained an advantage over us and came out against us in the field, but we drove them back to the entrance of the gate. Then the archers shot at your servants from the wall. Some of the king's servants are dead, and your servant Uriah the Hittite is dead also." David said to the messenger, "Thus shall you say to Joab, 'Do not let this matter trouble you, for the sword devours now one and now another. Strengthen your attack against the city and overthrow it.' And encourage him."

When the wife of Uriah heard that Uriah her husband was dead, she lamented over her husband. And when the mourning was over, David sent and brought her to his house, and she became his wife and bore him a son. But the thing that David had done displeased the Lord.

And the Lord sent Nathan to David. He came to him and said to him, "There were two men in a certain city, the one rich and the other poor. The rich man had very many flocks and herds, but the poor man had nothing but one little ewe lamb, which he had bought. And he brought it up, and it grew up with him and with his children. It used to eat of his morsel and drink from his cup and lie in his arms, and it was like a daughter to him. Now there came a traveler to the rich man, and he was unwilling to take one of his own flock or herd to prepare for the guest who had come to him, but he took the poor man's lamb and prepared it for the man who had come to him." Then David's anger was greatly kindled against the man, and he said to Nathan, "As the Lord lives, the man who has done this deserves to die, and he shall restore the lamb fourfold, because he did this thing, and because he had no pity."

Nathan said to David, "You are the man! Thus says the Lord, the God of Israel, 'I anointed you king over Israel, and I delivered you out of the hand of Saul. And I gave you your master's house and your master's wives into your arms and gave you the house of Israel and of Judah. And if this were too little, I would add to you as much more. Why have you despised the word of the Lord, to do what is evil in his sight? You have struck down Uriah the Hittite with the sword and have taken his wife to be your wife and have killed him with the sword of the Ammonites. Now therefore the sword shall never depart from your house, because you have despised me and have taken the wife of Uriah the Hittite to be your wife.' Thus says the Lord, 'Behold, I will raise up evil against you out of your own house. And I will take your wives before your eyes and give them to your neighbor, and he shall lie with your wives in the sight of this sun. For you did it secretly, but I will do this thing before all Israel and before the sun.'" David said to Nathan, "I have sinned against the Lord." And Nathan said to David, "The Lord also has put away your sin; you shall not die."

—2 SAMUEL 11:1–12:13

The Story of David and God

To the choirmaster. A Psalm of David, when Nathan the prophet went to him, after he had gone in to Bathsheba.

Have mercy on me, O God,
    according to your steadfast love;
according to your abundant mercy
    blot out my transgressions.
Wash me thoroughly from my iniquity,
    and cleanse me from my sin!

For I know my transgressions,
and my sin is ever before me.
Against you, you only, have I sinned
and done what is evil in your sight,
so that you may be justified in your words
and blameless in your judgment.
Behold, I was brought forth in iniquity,
and in sin did my mother conceive me.
Behold, you delight in truth in the inward being,
and you teach me wisdom in the secret heart.

Purge me with hyssop, and I shall be clean;
wash me, and I shall be whiter than snow.
Let me hear joy and gladness;
let the bones that you have broken rejoice.
Hide your face from my sins,
and blot out all my iniquities.
Create in me a clean heart, O God,
and renew a right spirit within me.
Cast me not away from your presence,
and take not your Holy Spirit from me.
Restore to me the joy of your salvation,
and uphold me with a willing spirit.

Then I will teach transgressors your ways,
and sinners will return to you.
Deliver me from bloodguiltiness, O God,
O God of my salvation,
and my tongue will sing aloud of your righteousness.
O Lord, open my lips,
and my mouth will declare your praise.
For you will not delight in sacrifice, or I would give it;
you will not be pleased with a burnt offering.
The sacrifices of God are a broken spirit;
a broken and contrite heart, O God, you will not despise.

Do good to Zion in your good pleasure;
build up the walls of Jerusalem;
then will you delight in right sacrifices,
in burnt offerings and whole burnt offerings;
then bulls will be offered on your altar.

—PSALM 51

Meditations

1 | Mercy Me: Psalm 51 and Everyday Life

Have mercy on me, O God, according to your
steadfast love; according to your abundant mercy
blot out my transgressions.

PSALM 51:1

It was one of those moments you want to take back. It was one of those times when you go where your desires and emotions are leading you. It was one of those situations when you know you should stop or walk away but feel you can't. And it was one of those moments when afterward you are confronted with the sin that still lives inside of you. Yes, it was one of those moments.

It wasn't a big deal in one way. Just a small conversation that had turned a bit ugly. It wasn't a dramatic life-altering moment. It was in the privacy of my home with one of my family members. But maybe that's the point. Perhaps it's very important because that's where I live every day. You see, you and I don't live in a series of big, dramatic moments. We don't careen from big decision to big decision. We all live in an endless series of little moments. The character of a life isn't set in ten big moments. The character of a life is set in ten thousand little moments of everyday life. It's the themes of struggles that emerge from those little moments that reveal what's really going on in our hearts.

So, I knew I couldn't back away from this little moment. I knew I had to own my sin. The minute I thought this, an inner struggle began. "I wasn't the only one at fault. If he hadn't said what he said, I wouldn't have become angry. I was actually pretty patient for much of the conversation." These were some of the arguments I was giving myself.

Isn't this interesting. Rather than appealing to the mercy of the Lord in the face of my sin, what I actually do instead is function as my own defense lawyer and present a list of arguments for my own righteousness. The theology behind the defense is that my greatest problem is outside of me, not inside of me. In so arguing, I'm telling myself that I don't really need to be rescued by the Lord's mercy. No, I'm telling myself that what I need to be rescued from is that sinner in the room who caused me to respond as I did.

Here's the point. Before you can ever make a clean and un-amended confession of your sin, you have to first begin by confessing your righteousness. It's not just your sin that separates you from God; your righteousness does as well. Because, when you are convinced you are righteous, you don't seek the forgiving, rescuing, and restoring mercy that can be found only in Jesus Christ.

What's actually true is that when I come to the Lord after I've blown it, I've only one argument to make. It's not the argument of the difficulty of the environment that I am in. It's not the argument of the difficult people that I'm near. It's not the argument of good intentions that were thwarted in some way. No, I have only one argument. It's right there in the first verse of Psalm 51, as David confesses his sin with Bathsheba. I come to the Lord with only one appeal, his mercy. I've no other defense. I've no other standing. I've no other hope. I can't escape the reality of my biggest problem—me! So I appeal to the one thing in my life that's sure and will never fail. I appeal to the one thing that guaranteed not only my acceptance with God, but the hope of new beginnings and fresh starts. I appeal on the basis of the greatest gift I ever have or ever will be given. I leave the courtroom of my own defense, I come out of hiding, and I admit who I am. But I'm not afraid, because I've been personally and eternally blessed. Because of what Jesus did, God looks on me with mercy. It's my only appeal; it's the source of my hope; it's my life. Mercy, mercy me!

Take a Moment

1. When you go to God in prayer, do you go as your own defense lawyer or as the guilty party (see Luke 18:9–14)? Do you tend to stack up arguments for your acceptability before God?

2. If you more quickly rested in God's mercy and, because of this, more readily admitted your sin, what practical changes in your life would result?

2 | On Being Sustained

Restore to me the joy of your salvation, and uphold
me with a willing spirit.

PSALM 51:12

It's a curious phrase: "and uphold me with a willing spirit."
What does it mean to be upheld with a willing spirit? What is it that
David prays for here and how does it fit with the confession that
makes up the rest of this remarkable psalm?

Human beings are simply not self-sustaining, and we were never
designed to live as if we are. The doctrine of creation confronts us with
the reality that we are neither physically nor spiritually self-sustaining.
We were created to be dependent. Dependency is not therefore a
sign of weakness. Rather it is a universal indicator of our humanity.
Humans are dependent beings. Yet we do not like to be dependent. It
is the legacy of our fallenness to do everything we can to conceptually
and functionally repudiate the doctrine of human dependency.

So, all fallen human beings tend to buy into two attractive but
dangerous lies. These are the lies that were on the tongue of the
serpent on that fateful day of manipulation and disobedience in the
garden. The first lie is the lie of autonomy, which tells me that I am
an independent human being with the right to invest my life however
I choose. The second lie is the lie of self-sufficiency, which declares
that I have everything I need within myself to be what I am supposed
to be and do what I am supposed to do. Because we do not want to
live for God, but for ourselves, we are easily seduced, at the mundane,
everyday level, by these lies.

But David now has his eyes open. He sees the lies for what they
are. He had wanted his own way. He had opted for independence.
He had stepped outside of God's boundaries. He had used his power
in the service of his own kingdom rather than God's. And it had all

23

been exposed and came crashing down around his feet. David had tried the path of independent self-sustenance. Psalm 51 is his prayer of repentance.

God has promised to sustain us by his grace. He has promised us the sustaining grace of forgiveness, so that we can stand before him unafraid. He has promised the sustaining grace of enablement, giving us the strength to do what he calls us to do. He has promised us the sustaining grace of protection, delivering us from evil. He has promised us the sustaining grace of wisdom, protecting us from our own foolishness. He has promised us the sustaining grace of perseverance, keeping us until the final enemy has been defeated. He has promised the sustaining grace of eternity, giving us the hope of a day when the struggle will be over.

It is a willing heart that causes us to seek the grace that has been promised. When we turn from our own way and recognize our inability to live his way, we begin to seek the full range of resources that he has promised us in his Son. Grace is for the willing and we only become willing when we confess not only the gravity of our sin, but our inability to deliver ourselves from it. Then our willingness opens to us all the sustenance of heart that can only be found in the Son.

Take a Moment

1. Where in your life have you opted for independence? In what ways are you not taking advantage of God's resources of help?

2. In what places do you need to rely more on the grace of Christ and the resources of help he has placed in your life (receiving loving confrontation well, seeking more honest fellowship in the body of Christ, more willingness to confess need to God and others)?

3 | Something in My Hands I Bring

....

The sacrifices of God are a broken spirit; a broken
and contrite heart, O God, you will not despise.

PSALM 51:17

God doesn't want you to come to Him empty-handed.
No, you can't come to Him full of yourself,
And you can't come to Him based on your track record
And you can't use your performance as a recommendation.
No, you can't come to Him based on your family,
Your personality,
Your education,
Your position in life,
The successes you've had,
The possessions you've accumulated,
Or the human acceptance you've gained.
But God requires you to come with your hands full.
He requires you to bring to Him the sweetest of sacrifices,
The sacrifice of words,
He calls you to bring Hosea's offering.
"Return, O Israel, to the LORD your God.
Your sins have been your downfall!
Take words with you
And return to the LORD.
Say to Him
'Forgive all our sins
And receive us graciously,
That we may offer our lips as the sacrifice of bulls.'"[1]
God doesn't want you to come to him empty-handed.
He asks of you a sacrifice.
Not a grain offering,
Not a lamb or a bull.

------

[1]Quotes in "Something in My Hands I Bring" are from Hosea 14:1–3 (AT).

No, that requirement has been satisfied
By the blood of the Lamb.
Yet God asks of you a sacrifice
It is the offering of words,
Words of humility,
Words of honesty,
Words of moral courage,
Words of moral candor,
Words that could only be spoken,
By one who rests in grace.
Words of confession are what you must bring.
Place words,
Free of negotiation or excuse,
On His altar of grace,
And receive forgiveness and cleansing.
Uncover your heart,
Exposed by words, and say:
"We will never again say, 'Our gods'
To what our own hands have made,
For in You the fatherless find compassion."
What David willingly did He requires of you,
Come with words,
It is the way of grace,
It is the way of freedom,
It is the way to God.

Take a Moment

1. What "word" sacrifice is God calling you to bring to him? Where do you need to seek the grace of forgiveness?

2. Is there a place where you are saying "our gods" to what your hands have made? What thing(s) in the creation tend to compete in your heart with the place that the Creator alone should occupy (a possession, position, person, circumstance, relationship, personal dream)?

4 | Big Grace

Behold, I was brought forth in iniquity, and in sin did my mother conceive me.

PSALM 51:5

What a devastating and hard-to-swallow description! Maybe you had it happen to you? A friend tells you he wants to talk to you, and when you get together, you realize that what he really wanted to do was confront you. You're not really excited about being told bad things about yourself, but this is your friend, so you're willing to listen. As he begins to lay out his concerns, you begin to feel pain inside. You can't believe what you're being told about yourself. Silently and inwardly you begin to rise to your own defense. You marshal arguments that you're a better person than the one being described. You want to believe that what you're hearing is a distortion, lacking in accuracy and love, but you know you can't. You're devastated because deep down you know it's true. Deep down you know that God has brought this person your way. Deep down you know what you're being required to consider is an accurate description of yourself.

Such a description is found in Genesis 6:5, "The LORD saw that the wickedness of man was great on the earth, and that every intention of the thoughts of his heart was only evil continually." What a devastating description! It's hard to swallow, isn't it? You want to think that this biblical description is of the people who are more sinful sinners than you and I are. But this verse is not describing a super-sinner class. No, it's a mirror into which every human being is meant to look and see himself. It is capturing in a few powerful words what theologians call "total depravity." Now, total depravity doesn't mean that as sinners we are as bad as we could possibly be. No, what it actually means is that sin reaches to every aspect of our personhood. Its damage of us is total. Physically, emotionally, intellectually, spiritually, motivationally, socially, we have been damaged by sin. Its ravages are inescapable and comprehensive. No one has dodged its scourge, and no one has been partially affected. We are all sinners. It reaches to every aspect of what makes us *us*. Sadly, when each of us looks into the mirror of Genesis 6:5, we see an accurate description of ourselves.

Now, you have to ask yourself: Why is Genesis 6:5 so hard to accept? Why do we spontaneously rise to our own defense? Why are you and I devastated when our weakness, sin, and failure are pointed out? Why do we find confrontation and rebuke painful even when they are done in love? Why do we want to believe that we are in the good class of sinners? Why do we want to believe that we are deprived, but not depraved? Or that we are depraved, but not totally? Why do we find comfort in pointing to people who appear to be worse sinners than we are? Why do we make up self-atoning revisions of our own history? Why do we erect self-justifying arguments for what we have said or done? Why do we turn the tables when someone points out a wrong, making sure that they know that we know that we're not the only sinner in the room? Why do we line up all the good things we've done as a counter-balance for the wrong that is being highlighted? Why is this all so hard to accept?

There's only one answer to all of these questions. There's only one conclusion that fits. We find this all so hard to accept because we studiously hold onto the possibility that we're more righteous than the Bible describes us to be. When we look into the mirror of self-appraisal, the person we tend to see is a person who is more righteous than any of us actually is!

We were at the end of a wonderful service at Tenth Presbyterian Church that had been punctuated by a powerful sermon from the Ten Commandments. I immediately turned to my wife at the end of the service and said, "I am so glad our children were here to hear that sermon!" She didn't even have to say anything to me. She simply gave me that look. You know, the one that says, "I can't believe you are actually saying what you are saying." Immediately I felt embarrassed and grieved. It had happened to me so subtly and quickly. I had placed myself outside of the circle of the sermon's diagnosis. I had accepted the fact that whatever Exodus and Phil Ryken were describing did not include me. And I was glad that the people in my family who really needed the diagnosis had been in attendance.

"Therefore, since we have been justified by faith, we have peace with God through our Lord Jesus Christ. Through him we have also obtained access by faith into this grace in which we stand, and we rejoice in hope of the glory of God" (Romans 5:1–2). If the Bible's description is accurate, then God's grace is our only hope. Thank God that he has given us big grace! Each one of us needs grace that's not only big enough to forgive our sin, but also powerful enough to free us from the self-atoning prison of our own righteousness. We're not only held captive by our sin, but also by the delusion of our righteousness. Resting in God's grace isn't just about confessing your sin; it's about forsaking your righteousness as well. So we all need the big grace that's found only in the person and work of the Lord Jesus Christ.

We must all, with humility, say to the God of big grace, "Behold, I was brought forth in iniquity, and in sin did my mother conceive me. . . . Wash me thoroughly from my iniquity, and cleanse me from my sin!" (Psalm 51:5, 2). And then rest in his righteousness alone.

Take a Moment

1. Is there a possibility that you are not resting in the righteousness you have been given in Christ because you are seeing yourself as more righteous than you actually are? Where in your life do you tend to take too much pride in your wisdom, maturity, and performance rather than resting in the big grace you have found in Jesus?

2. How do you typically respond when personal sin, weakness, failure, foolishness, or immaturity is pointed out to you? Where do you tend to erect self-justifying arguments for your words or behavior?

5 | A Rabbi and Two Imams

Have mercy on me, O God, according to your
steadfast love.

PSALM 51:1

It was a wonderful opportunity. I was asked to participate in
an open discussion about death and dying from a patient's perspective. The event was held at a local medical college. It was the first
ministry situation I had ever been in where I had sat between a rabbi
and two imams. My Jewish and Islamic colleagues were all very warm
and articulate, but I had an unfair advantage: I came armed with the
gospel. I carried something into the room that no one else had, and
as the evening went on this message glistened with greater and greater
beauty.

The men on either side of me were gentle and caring. They knew
their faith well, but they had one distinct disadvantage: the only message they brought into the room was the message of the law. The only
hope they could give was the hope that somehow, someway, a person
could be obedient enough to be accepted into eternity with God. The
more they spoke, the more beautiful the gospel looked.

The most significant moment of the evening came when we were
asked about what we would say to a family of someone who had
committed suicide. It was at this moment that the gospel shined the
brightest. I said, "Suicide doesn't change the paradigm. Think with
me: who of us could lie in our bed during the last hours of our life and
look back and say to ourselves that we have been as good as a person
could be? Wouldn't all of us look back and have regrets about things
we have chosen, said, and done? None of us is able to commend ourselves to God on the basis of our performance. In this way, the person
who has committed suicide and the person who hasn't are exactly the

same. Both of them are completely dependent on the forgiveness of a God of grace, in order to have any hope for eternity."

You and I share identity with the hypothetical suicidal man just as we share identity with the adulterous and murderous king of Psalm 51. Our only hope is one thing—God's "steadfast love" and his "abundant mercy" (v. 1). We cannot look to our education, or family, or ministry track record, or our theological knowledge, or our evangelistic zeal, or our faithful obedience. We have one hope; it is the hope to which this ancient psalm looks. Here is that hope in the words of a wonderful old hymn, "Jesus Paid It All":

> Since nothing good have I
> Whereby Thy grace to claim,
> I'll wash my garment white
> In the blood of Calvary's lamb.

> Jesus paid it all,
> All to Him I owe;
> Sin had left a crimson stain;
> He washed it white as snow.

I said good-bye to the rabbi and the two imams and got in my car to drive home. But I didn't just drive; I celebrated! I was very excited as I thought about the evening, not because I had had such a golden opportunity to speak the gospel, but because by means of God's grace I had been included in it!

Take a Moment

1. What are the things in life that you regularly celebrate (new job, birthday, holidays, a certain accomplishment)? Do you celebrate the amazing grace of God that has been given you through his Son the Lord Jesus Christ?

2. Do you really believe that your only hope in life is found in God's grace? Is your daily habit to admit that there is nothing you have done or could ever do to earn or deserve the blessings that you have been given? Is your life more characterized by thankfulness or complaint?

6 | Accurate Self-assessment

For I know my transgressions, and my sin is ever
before me.

PSALM 51:3

Sin lives in a costume; that's why it's so hard to recognize. The
fact that sin looks so good is one of the things that make it so bad.
In order for it to do its evil work, it must present itself as something
that is anything but evil. Life in a fallen world is like attending the
ultimate masquerade party. Impatient yelling wears the costume of a
zeal for truth. Lust can masquerade as a love for beauty. Gossip does
its evil work by living in the costume of concern and prayer. Craving
for power and control wears the mask of biblical leadership. Fear of
man gets dressed up as a servant heart. The pride of always being
right masquerades as a love for biblical wisdom. Evil simply doesn't
present itself as evil, which is part of its draw.

You'll never understand sin's sleight of hand until you acknowledge that the DNA of sin is deception. Now, what this means
personally is that as sinners we are all very committed and gifted self-
swindlers. I say all the time to people that no one is more influential in
their own lives than they themselves are because no one talks to them
more than they themselves do. We're all too skilled at looking at our
own wrong and seeing good. We're all much better at seeing the sin,
weakness, and failure of others than we are our own. We're all very
good at being intolerant of others of the very things that we willingly
tolerate in ourselves. The bottom line is that sin causes us not to hear
or see ourselves with accuracy. And we not only tend to be blind, but,
to compound matters, we also tend to be blind to our blindness.

What does all of this mean? It means that accurate self-assess-
ment is the product of grace. It is only in the mirror of God's Word
and with the sight-giving help of the Holy Spirit that we are able to

see ourselves as we actually are. In those painful moments of accurate self-sight, we may not feel as if we are being loved, but that is exactly what is happening. God, who loves us enough to sacrifice his Son for our redemption, works so that we would see ourselves clearly, so that we would not buy into the delusion of our own righteousness, and so that with a humble sense of personal need we would seek the resources of grace that can only be found in him.

In this way, Psalm 51 is both the saddest and most joyous of all the psalms. It is sad that David has to confess what he must confess, but at the same time the fact that he is accurately seeing, and fully acknowledging his sin is a cause for celebration. Only Jesus can open blind eyes. Whenever a sinner accurately assesses his sin, the angels in heaven rejoice, and so should we.

Take a Moment

1. Do you pray for open eyes to see yourself more clearly? Is your confidence in Christ so firm that you are unafraid to pray that God would free you from your own patterns of self-swindling that keep you blind and inhibit your growth?

2. Stop and take time to thank God for his loving zeal to use Scripture, others, and the situations of life to reveal you to yourself so that you may continue to grow and change by his grace.

7 | Violent Grace

Let the bones that you have broken rejoice.

PSALM 51:8

Our relationship with the Lord is never anything other than a relationship of grace. It is grace that brought us into his family. It is grace that keeps us in it, and it is grace that will continue us in it forever. But the grace that we have been given is not always comfortable grace. Here is why.

As sinners we all become way too comfortable with our sin. The thought that once bothered becomes an action that no longer plagues our conscience. The word that troubled us the first time it was uttered now is accompanied by others that are worse. The marriage that was once a picture of biblical love has now become a relationship of cold-war detente. Commitment to work degenerates into doing as little as we can for as much pay as we can negotiate. A commitment to a devotional life becomes perfunctory and empty duty, more like getting our ticket punched for heaven than enjoying communion with our Lord. Minor, unexpressed irritation, which once troubled our hearts, is now fully expressed anger that is easily rationalized away. Sin is like the unnoticed drips of water that silently destroy the foundation of a house.

You see, we all have a perverse capacity to be comfortable with what God says is wrong. So God blesses us with violent, uncomfortable grace. Yes, he really does love us enough to crush us, so that we would feel the pain of our sin and run to him for forgiveness and deliverance. David says, "Let the bones that you have broken rejoice" (v. 8). It is a curious phrase. Crushed bones and rejoicing don't seem to go together. You wouldn't say, "Hooray, I have a broken bone!" But that is very close to what David is saying. He is using the searing pain of broken bones as a metaphor of the pain of heart that you feel when you really see your sin for what it is. That pain is a good thing.

Think about it: the physical pain of an actual broken bone is worth being thankful for because it's a warning sign something is wrong in that arm or leg. In the same way, God's loving hammer of conviction is meant to break your heart, and the pain of heart you feel is meant to alert you to the fact that something is spiritually wrong inside of you. Like the warning signal of physical pain, the rescuing and restoring pain of convicting grace is a thing worth celebrating.

So God's grace isn't always comfortable because he isn't primarily working on our comfort; he's working on our character. With violent grace he will crush us because he loves us and is committed to our restoration, deliverance, and refinement. And that is something worth celebrating.

Take a Moment

1. Have you allowed yourself to become comfortable with something that God does not want to have bring you comfort?

2. Is there a place in your life where you have been tempted to doubt God's love because you are experiencing the pain of his rescuing and restoring grace? Stop and thank him for violent grace that rescues you from yourself.

8 | Aren't You Glad You're Not Like David?

To the choirmaster. A Psalm of David, when Nathan the prophet went to him, after he had gone in to Bathsheba.

TITLE OF PSALM 51

Aren't you glad you're not like David,
Such blazoned sin, how could he?
Aren't you glad you're not like Saul,
Making up his own rules; what was he thinking?
Aren't you glad you're not like Cain,
Violence against his own brother?
Aren't you glad you're not like Rebekah,
Such planned deceit?
Aren't you glad you're not like the Israelites,
So easily seduced by idols?
Aren't you glad you're not like Absalom;
How could he be so jealous?
Aren't you glad you're not like Elijah;
How could he forget God, be so depressed?
Aren't you glad you're not like Nebuchadnezzar;
How could he be so obsessed with power?
Aren't you glad you're not like Samson;
How could he be so easily deceived?
Aren't you glad you're not like Jonah;
How could he run from the Father's call?
Aren't you glad you're not like the Pharisees,
So religiously right yet spiritually wrong?
Aren't you glad you're not like Judas,
Selling the Messiah for a little bit of silver?
Aren't you glad you're not like the Corinthians,
So much better at division than at serving the Lord?

But wait.
You are like them, and so am I.
There is simply no denying it.
Their stories are a mirror into which we see ourselves.
We too are jealous and easily deceived.
We too are proud and obsessed with power.
We are better at division while we run from God.
We too get angry and get seduced by idols.
In sorrow we must say,
We stand with David,
And Saul,
And Rebekah,
And Jonah,
And Elijah,
And the rest.
These stories are for us to look into and see us,
so that we are not able,
to buy into,
the lie of our own righteousness.
But instead,
Run to His mercy,
Hold onto His unfailing love,
and finally rest,
In His great compassion.
Aren't you glad you can step out of the darkness of self-deceit,
and admit who you are?

Take a Moment

1. When you read the Bible, do you intentionally try to use it as a mirror that is able to show you as you actually are?

2. Do you humbly identify with the weakness, foolishness, and failure of the characters of Scripture, or do you tend to tell yourself that you are essentially different from them?

9 | No More "If Only"

> Behold, I was brought forth in iniquity, and in sin did
> my mother conceive me.
>
> PSALM 51:5

It's so easy to slip into an "if only" lifestyle. I find myself slipping into it often. The "if only" possibilities are endless:

If only I'd been from a more stable family.
If only I'd had better friends as I was growing up.
If only my parents had sent me to better schools.
If only I'd been given better intellectual gifts.
If only that accident hadn't happened.
If only I'd had better physical health.
If only that degree program had been as good as advertised.
If only I'd been able to find a better job.
If only I didn't have to fight the traffic every day.
If only I'd been able to get married.
If only I hadn't gotten married so young.
If only I'd understood marriage more before I got married.
If only I had a more understanding spouse.
If only I'd come to know Christ earlier.
If only I'd found a good church when I was young.
If only I didn't have to struggle with my finances.
If only it was easier and more comfortable for me to communicate
    with others.
If only I could find a small group that I could be comfortable with.
If only I could have had children.
If only my children were more obedient.
If only I knew the Bible better.
If only that boss hadn't fired me.
If only I had a better place to live.
If only I could find some place where I feel like I really belong.
If only God seemed closer to me.

If only I didn't have to work so hard to make ends meet.
If only . . .

The seductive thing about our "if onlys" is that there is a bit of plausibility in all of them. We do live in a fallen world. We all face hardships of various kinds. We all have been sinned against in a variety of ways. None of us has ever lived in ideal circumstances or in perfect relationships. The world is a broken place and we have all been touched in many ways by its brokenness. Yet, the "if only" lifestyle tends to say, "My biggest problems in life exist outside of me and not inside of me."

In Psalm 51 David says something very radical. It is counter-intuitive to a culture that tends to say that we all are the result of what our experience has made us. David says, "Surely I have been a sinner from birth, sinful from the time my mother conceived me." David is saying that his greatest problem in all of life is not the result of what he has suffered in the situations and relationships of his life. Rather, David is saying that his biggest problem is internal and was there before he had any of these experiences. And David gives this deep and internal problem a name, sin. How humbling!

Think about it this way: it is the evil that is inside of you that either magnetizes you to the evil outside of you or causes you to deal with the evil outside of you in a way that is wrong. It is only when you begin to accept that your greatest problem in all of life is not what has happened or been done to you that you begin to get excited about the rescuing grace of Jesus Christ. It is only when you begin to accept that your greatest need is something with which you came into the world that you will begin to hunger for the help that only God can give you. It is only then that you will begin to hunger for more than changes of situation and relationship. It is only then that you will begin to accept the most radical and personally liberating truth that you could ever conceive. What is that truth? It is that what you and I really need to be rescued from is ourselves! We are the biggest danger to ourselves. That is why God offers us the gorgeous promise of his grace which has the power to change us from the inside out.

Are you embracing that promise or are you still saying, "If only . . ."?

Take a Moment

1. When you are dealing with the often difficult realities of life in this fallen world, what are the "if onlys" that tend to flood into your head?

2. Are there places where you tend to question whether God has given you what you need to do what he has called for you to do? What would change in your life if you really believed in the completeness and sufficiency of his provision for you?

10 | Something Bigger

> Then I will teach transgressors your ways, and
> sinners will return to you.
>
> PSALM 51:13

I have a confession to make. My confession is that I think I went for years as a Christian and didn't really understand confession. I think there's a subtle, yet significant, difference between the admission of wrong and true heart confession. Let me give you an example. Let's just say (and you know this would never happen in my marriage) that in a moment of busyness and irritation, I speak unkindly to my wife. And let's imagine that a friend overhears what I've said and comes to me and confronts me with this wrong. Now I've been caught. He heard my words; there's no way of escaping it. And so with him watching and Luella listening, I say, "You're right; I shouldn't have spoken that way. Luella, please forgive me." Now this doesn't sound so bad on the surface, but it bears examining.

I've admitted that what I said was wrong, and that's a good thing, but there are two potential flaws in this confession. The first is it could be that the only reason I admitted to this wrong was that I was caught red-handed. I may not have been grieved at all by what I'd said. I may have confessed simply because I was in trouble. The second flaw could be that the confession was only a confession of the behavior (and that's a good thing as far as it goes) but not a confession from the heart that's behind the behavior. Here's the point. It's only when I'm grieved by my sin and acknowledge that this sin is heart-deep that my confession will be followed by the turning of repentance. You see, I speak unkindly to my wife not because my schedule is busy or because she's less than perfect, but because there are things that I want (such as success, control, approval) and when she gets in the way of these things, I'm immediately irritated.

When David, in Psalm 51, prays for a pure heart and a steadfast

41

spirit (vv. 10–11), he's acknowledging that his struggle with sin runs deeper than just behavior. He's not only confessing to the physical acts of adultery and murder, but also to the reality of a heart that's corrupt; that is, it loves personal pleasure more than it loves the Lord. When he talks of God's desire for a truthful and wise heart (v. 6), he's confessing to a heart that's craved what's impure and that's loved what's foolish.

What results when you confess because you're deeply grieved by what you've done? What happens when you acknowledge that your physical sin is caused by a heart that's run amuck? The result is that you turn, really turn. What do I mean? I mean that you don't just turn away from the physical sin pattern, but your heart turns to God in new and deeper ways. What does this mean? It means that rather than being driven by the craving for the delivery of your little kingdom desires by the people and circumstances around you, your heart begins to be motivated by big kingdom purposes. True confession always results in living for something bigger.

And so David, once obsessed with the temporary and impure pleasures of his claustrophobic little kingdom of one, now becomes excited with and engaged in the transcendent purposes of God's big-sky kingdom. So he says:

> Then I will teach transgressors your ways,
>   and sinners will return to you.
> Deliver me from bloodguiltiness,
>   O God, God of my salvation,
>   and my tongue will sing aloud of your righteousness.
> O Lord, open my lips,
>   and my mouth will declare your praise. (vv. 13–15)

A truly broken and contrite heart will always turn to live for something bigger. Is your confession leading you there?

Take a Moment

1. Do the things you confess tend to be limited to wrong words and wrong actions, or do you confess to the wrong thoughts and desires that lie behind the behavior or words?

2. Does your confession result in an excitement with living for something bigger than your own wants, needs, and feelings?

11 | Romans 7

Wash me thoroughly from my iniquity, and
cleanse me from my sin!

PSALM 51:2

I am a mass of contradictions; I don't want to be but I am.
I preach a gospel of peace, but my life isn't always driven by peace.
I talk about a Jesus who alone can fully satisfy the soul, but I am
    often not satisfied.
I celebrate a theology of amazing grace, but I often react in ungrace.
And if I rest in God's control, why do I seek it for myself?
Even in moments when I think I am prepared, I end up doing what
    I didn't want to do.
Irritation
Impatience
Envy
Discontent
Wrong talk
Anger
Self-focus
Are not the fruit of the new life, are not the way of grace.
So there is this law operating inside of me.
When I step out with a desire to do good, evil follows me wherever I go.
There is this war that rages inside of me, between a desire for good
    and sin that is anything but good.
There are times when I feel like a prisoner, held against my will.
I didn't plan to be mad in the grocery store, but that guy made me mad.
I didn't plan to be discontent, but it just enveloped me in the quietness
    of the car.
That discussion wasn't supposed to degenerate into an argument,
    but it did.
I am thankful for God's grace, but there is daily evidence that I'm still
    in need of help.
That battle inside me cannot be solved by

Theology
Strategies
Principles
Techniques
Plans
Preparation
Helpful hints
Outlines.
I have been humbled by the war I cannot win.
I have been grieved by desires I cannot conquer.
I have been confronted by actions I cannot excuse.
And I have come to confess that what I really need is rescue.
So, have mercy on me, O God,
According to Your unfailing love
According to Your great compassion
Blot out my transgressions.
Wash away all my iniquity
And cleanse me from my sin.
For I know my transgressions
And my sin is always before me.
I embrace the rescue that could only be found in You.
Thanks be to God—through Jesus Christ our Lord!

Take a Moment

1. Is there a place right now where how you live is not consistent with what you say you believe? Isn't it wonderful that you do not have to panic, hide, or be depressed? Stop and confess your inconsistency to the One who was consistent so that you could be accepted and forgiven even in your moments of greatest inconsistency.

2. What temptations tend to hook you again and again? Are you holding onto and celebrating the grace that you have been given that really is greater and more powerful than any sin that hooks you?

12 | Darkness and Light

For I know my transgressions.

PSALM 51:3

He'd lived in the darkness for so long he didn't know that it was dark. Dark was normal, and since he'd never experienced light, dark didn't seem dark to him. It wasn't as though he woke up in the morning praying and longing for light. And it wasn't that he had to work to accept the darkness. No, darkness was all he'd ever known. Sure, he fumbled around, bumped into things, and fell down a lot, but none of it bothered him. It was what every day was like for him. He didn't really long to see. He didn't long to see because he didn't know that there was anything worth seeing. He really did think that he saw all there was to see—darkness. He didn't have an accurate sense of size, shape, or color. He had little sense of beauty. He didn't really know what things looked like because the darkness he lived in was so pervasive that the objects around him were but shadows, blobs, and blurs.

He had no idea what he looked like because he'd never really seen himself. He thought he knew what he looked like because he'd touched his face and run his hands down his torso, but he'd never seen himself in the light. He was actually quite content in his darkened world, and he was quite happy to do what people do when they live in a dark place. He just got up every day and did what you do when you can't see. Except he didn't know that he couldn't see, because he'd never seen, because he'd always lived in darkness.

Then it happened one day. He hadn't longed for it. He hadn't asked for it. It just happened. A shaft of light exploded into his world. At first it scared and confused him. He didn't know what it was and his eyes didn't seem able to take it in. All he really knew was that it was different from the darkness he'd always known. It was bright

45

and beautiful and it hurt his eyes, but he couldn't stop looking. He couldn't keep himself from walking toward the light. The closer he got to the light, the more he began to see what was around him. There was a whole world of shapes and colors he'd never seen. But something even more profound began to happen to him. It was shocking, disturbing, and exciting all at once. The closer he got to the light, the more he saw himself! The first thing he realized was that he was naked. For the first time he felt naked. For the first time his nakedness made him uncomfortable. But he not only realized he was naked, he realized he was dirty. And not only was he dirty, he was confronted with the fact that he was lame.

He kept walking toward the light, and he felt joy as he did so, but the joy was mixed with grief. As he walked he began to weep. He'd never wept like this before. He wept at the pain he felt over his condition. He'd not known how dirty he was. He'd not known how crippled he was, and he felt overwhelmed at what he now knew. He was stunned by the fact that he'd been this way since birth and he'd never known it. He was shocked that he'd never figured out that he moved with a limp. But his shock was quickly mixed with the deepest longing he'd ever felt. It was like he was starved for something he'd never eaten but now wanted desperately. What he wanted desperately for the first time in his life was to be clean. For the first time in his life he wasn't satisfied being crippled. He longed to be healed. And even though he didn't understand light at all, for the first time in his life he wanted to live in it. And he couldn't imagine ever being content to live in the darkness again.

So he started to run. He ran because he felt drawn—drawn to the light that had so radically altered his world. He wanted to be in the light because somehow he knew that if he could get in the light, he'd be washed and he'd be clean. Somehow he knew that if he could get to the light he would be healed. He'd never run before because he knew he couldn't run because he was lame, but he did run. The light was drawing him. The light was giving him strength.

He remembers well those darkened days in that darkened place. He remembers it all with a broken and a celebratory heart. And he is very aware that not only has he been cleansed and healed, he's been given the ability to see as well. And he's deeply grateful that he's been clothed with what he couldn't purchase and that deep within him has been placed the desire to be clean.

> Generous in love—God, give grace!
> Huge in mercy—wipe out my bad record.
> Scrub away my guilt,
> soak out my sins in your laundry.
> I know how bad I've been;
> my sins are staring me down. (Psalm 51:1–3 MESSAGE)

Take a Moment

1. By his amazing grace God has freed you from darkness and freed you to live in the light of his love and truth. Where are you still tempted or attracted to the darkness (an old habit, a previous relationship, a secret desire, a troubling pattern of thought)?

2. What changes has God brought into your life that you need to see, to remember, to celebrate, and to pursue?

13 | The Dance of Redemption

Restore to me the joy of your salvation.

PSALM 51:12

My sin
Your unfailing love.
My transgression
Your great compassion.
My iniquity
Your cleansing.
My evil
Your mercy.
My sin
Your wisdom.
My iniquity
Your presence.
My transgression
Your restoration.
My sin
Your salvation.
My song
Your righteousness.
My broken heart
Your delight.
My prosperity
Your good pleasure.
Your altar
my delight.
Hide Your face
from my sins
Create in me
a pure heart
Do not
cast me from Your presence

Do not
take Your Spirit from me
Restore to me
the joy of your salvation
Grant me
a willing spirit
Save me
from bloodguilt
Sustain me.
For I know
my transgressions
And my sin
is ever before me.

Take a Moment

1. Because of God's love, you have been invited to the dance of redemption. In the middle of the dance, what are the things that you pray for the most? Do they tend to have to do with situations and circumstances more than they have to do with struggles of the heart?

2. Right here, right now, where do you need to pray for God's help, power, rescue, love, and wisdom?

14 | Sin—It's Everywhere, It's Everywhere!

My sin is ever before me.

PSALM 51:3

"Sin is not hurtful because it is forbidden, but forbidden because it is hurtful."

BENJAMIN FRANKLIN

"Marriage is three parts love and seven parts forgiveness of sin."

LAO TZU

"Other men's sins are before our eyes; our own are behind our backs."

SENECA

"Pleasure is the bait of sin."

PLATO

"A sin takes on new and real terror when there seems to be a chance that it is going to be found out."

MARK TWAIN

"Do not bite at the bait of pleasure till you know there is no hook beneath it."

THOMAS JEFFERSON

"Sin is sweet in the beginning, but bitter in the end."

THE TALMUD

"Laziness grows on people; it begins in cobwebs and ends in iron chains."

THOMAS FOWELL BUXTON

"To sin is a human business, to justify sins is a devilish business."

TOLSTOY

"If you have sinned, do not lie down without repentance; for the want of repentance after one has sinned makes the heart harder and harder."

JOHN BUNYAN

"The beginning of atonement is the sense of its necessity."

LORD BYRON

"It is impossible for a man to be freed from the habit of sin before he hates it, just as it is impossible to receive forgiveness before confessing his trespasses."

IGNATIUS

"We have a strange illusion that mere time cancels sin. But mere time does nothing either to the fact or the guilt of sin."

C. S. LEWIS

"Self is the root, the tree, and the branches of all the evils of our fallen state."

WILLIAM LAW

"In short, a man must be free from the sin he is, which makes him do the sin he does."

GEORGE MACDONALD

"The temptation of the age is to look good without being good."

BRENNAN MANNING

"Repentance is but a denying of our will, and an opposition of our fantasies."

MONTAIGNE

"Personal sin reflected upon breeds compassion."

JOHN M. SHANAHAN

"People don't do what they believe in—they just do what's most convenient and then they repent."

BOB DYLAN

"I would rather feel remorse than know how to define it."

THOMAS À KEMPIS

"Why does no one confess his sins? Because he is yet in them. It is for a man who has awoke from sleep to tell his dreams."

SENECA

"All sins tend to be addictive, and the terminal point of addiction is damnation."

W. H. AUDEN

"Adam ate the apple, and our teeth still ache."

HUNGARIAN PROVERB

"Sin is never at a stay; if we do not retreat from it, we shall advance in it, and the farther we go, the more we have to come back."

ISAAC BARROW

"Out of timber so crooked as that from which man is made nothing entirely straight can be built."

EMMANUEL KANT

"We are all too Christian to really enjoy sinning, and all too fond of sin to really enjoy Christianity."

PETER MARSHALL

"Original sin is that thing about man which makes him capable of conceiving of his own perfection and incapable of achieving it."

REINHOLD NIEBUHR

"Few love to hear the sins they love to act."

WILLIAM SHAKESPEARE

Take a Moment

1. What fresh things does God want you to learn and remember about sin?

2. How should these new insights change the way you approach the situations and relationships of your daily life?

15 | Sinners and Unafraid

... according to your steadfast love;
according to your abundant mercy.

PSALM 51:1

The older you get the more you move from being an astronaut to an archaeologist. When you're young, you're excitedly launching to worlds unknown. You have all of the major decisions of life before you, and you can spend your time assessing your potential and considering opportunities. It's a time of exploration and discovery. It's a time to go where you've never been before and to do what you've never done. It's a time to begin to use your training and to gain experience.

But as you get older, you begin to look back at least as much as you look forward. As you look back, you tend to dig through the mound of the civilization that was your past life, looking for pottery shards of thoughts, desires, choices, actions, words, decisions, relationships, and situations. And as you do this, you can't help but assess how you have done with what you have been given.

Now let's think about this for a moment. Who would be so arrogant and bold as to look back on their life and say, "In every possible way I was as good as I could have been"? Wouldn't we all hold some of those pottery shards in our hands and experience at least a bit of regret? Wouldn't all of us wish that we could take back words we have said, decisions we have made, or actions we have taken?

Here's what all of this means: if you and I are at all willing to humbly and honestly look at our lives, we will be forced to conclude that we are flawed human beings. And yet we don't have to beat ourselves up. We don't have to work to minimize or deny our failures. We don't have to be defensive when our weaknesses are revealed. We don't have to rewrite our own histories to make ourselves look better than we actually were. We don't have to be paralyzed by remorse and regret. We don't have to distract ourselves with busyness or drug ourselves with substances. Isn't it wonderful that we can stare our deepest, darkest failures in the face and be unafraid? Isn't it comforting that we can honestly face our most regretful moments and not be devastated? Isn't it amazing that we can confess that we really are sinners and be neither fearful nor depressed?

Isn't it wonderful that we can do all of these things because, like David, we have learned that our hope in life is not in the purity of our character or the perfection of our performance. We can face that we are sinners and rest because we know that God really does exist and that he is a God of:

Mercy,
Steadfast love,
Abundant Mercy
Because he is, there is hope—hope of forgiveness and
    new beginnings.

Yes, we really can fully acknowledge our sin and failure and yet be unafraid.

Take a Moment

1. Are there places where your living still portrays an unhealthy fear of God's anger, judgment, and rejection? Do you ever doubt that he could love a person like you?

2. Is there a place in your life where you are still holding on to regret even though God has forgiven you and does not respond to you based on your past performance?

16 | The Gospel of Prosperity

> Do good to Zion in your good pleasure;
> build up the walls of Jerusalem.
>
> PSALM 51:18

It is an interesting way to conclude a prayer of humble confession:

> In your good pleasure make Zion prosper;
>   build up the walls of Jerusalem.
> Then there will be righteous sacrifices,
>   whole burnt offerings to delight you;
>   then bulls will be offered on your altar. (Psalm 51:18–19 NIV)

Yes, this prayer of confession really does end with a prayer for prosperity. David is so bold as to not only ask God for mercy, but also to ask God that he would bless him, and not only him but all of Israel! You may think, "Hasn't this man learned his lesson? After all of this, hasn't he learned what is really important?" But we need to look at this final piece of David's prayer again and this time more closely.

What David is requesting is completely different from the modern "health and wealth gospel" prayers for prosperity. Those prayers for prosperity have one fatal flaw in them. They are prayers for prosperity for the purpose of the delight of the person praying the prayer. Not so with David. He has lived a little, self-focused life. He has now been caught up in the call to live large, that is, for a kingdom greater than his own. This prayer is evidence that he's learned the lesson of the danger of living for his own delight. This prayer for prosperity is the result of a radically changed heart.

Why does David pray for prosperity? For one reason, he asks it for the glory and delight of the Lord. When God prospers people who are no longer living for their own little kingdoms but are living for his, the result is the furtherance of his kingdom purposes on earth, which results in his glory. Give wisdom to a man who is living for God's kingdom and he'll use that wisdom to advance God's kingdom. Give money to a man who loves God's kingdom and he'll look for ways to invest that money in kingdom causes. Give a house to a person who seeks God's kingdom and his house will be a place of hospitality, love, and ministry. David prays for prosperity, not for his glory but for the glory of the Lord to whom his heart has now turned.

But there's more. When people are blessed by the Lord they turn to him in humble, sacrificial worship. It's in those moments when I am cogently aware of God's forgiveness and gratefully aware of his undeserved blessing that I willingly offer to him what I would have once held to tightly. God delights in the sacrifices of his people, because when they are worshiping him in this way, they are doing the thing for which they were created. When I've quit looking for satisfaction in the created world and begin to find my satisfaction in the Lord, then I'm willing to hold loosely to the things that once held me. It's here that my delight is the Lord's delight.

So is it right to pray for prosperity? It is and you should, not for the sake of your kingdom, but for the success of his. Not for the sake of your delight, but for his. You see, when God prospers people who are living for him, they use that blessing to serve him all the more, and for this he gets glory and in this he finds great delight.

Take a Moment

1. What kind of blessing do you crave? What are the "good things" that you wish God would give you? If you had your way, how would God prosper you?

2. How *do* you hold the blessings God gives you? How do you tend to use the things that he has entrusted to your care?

17 | Somebody Else

... so that you may be justified in your words
and blameless in your judgment.

PSALM 51:4

I really wish I could blame
somebody else.
I wish I could place the responsibility
on somebody else.
I would love to point the finger
at somebody else.
I wish I could convince myself
that it was somebody else.
I tried to feed myself the logic
that it was somebody else.
For a moment I bought my argument
that it was somebody else.
There is always another sinner
who can bear my fault.
There is always some circumstance
that can carry my blame.
There's always some factor
that made me do what I did.
There's always somewhere else to point
rather than looking at me.
But in the darkness of bedtime
the logic melts out of my heart.
In the moments before sleep
the pain begins to squeeze away my breath.
As my mind replays the day's moments
the conclusion is like a slap.
There is no monster
to hide from.
There is no excuse that holds.

My war is not external,
the enemy is not outside.
The struggle rages within me,
nowhere to point or run.
No independent righteousness,
no reason for smugness or rest.
I am my greatest enemy
and rescue my only hope.
In the quiet I face it
I cannot blame somebody else.
One more time I close my eyes admitting
my only hope is found in Somebody else.

Take a Moment

1. Are there places where you have been tempted to blame inside (heart) struggles on outside pressures? ("He makes me so jealous!" "This traffic makes me so angry!" "I wasn't this irritable until I got this job.")

2. Where have you failed to seek the grace that is yours as God's child because you have successfully told yourself that your biggest, most abiding problem is outside, not inside, of you?

18 | Unfailing Love

For you will not delight in sacrifice, or
I would give it; you will not be pleased with
a burnt offering.

PSALM 51:16

I wish I would live with You in view;
Eyes to Your glory
Ears for Your wisdom
Heart for Your grace.
But I live with me in view.
Eyes to my kingdom
Ears for my opinion
Heart captured by my will.
I know I was made for You,
I know that Hope
Meaning
Purpose
Identity
My agenda for every day,
Is to be found in You.
But I want my own kingdom
I love my own glory
I define my own meaning
I delight in my control.
I know You are not fooled
By my burnt offerings.
There's a war that never ends;
The battleground is my heart.
It's a moral skirmish
Between what You have ordained
And what I want.
So I don't find pleasure in Your glory,
I don't delight in Your law.

But my heart doesn't rest;
I know there's a better way.
I know You are God
And I am not.
My sin is more than
Bad behavior
A bad choice
Wrong words.
My sin is a violation of the relationship
That I was meant to have with You.
My sin is an act
Where I replace You
With something I love more.
Every wrong thing I do
Reflects
A lack of love for You,
Reflects
A love of self.
Help me
To see
To acknowledge
To weep
And say,
"Against You, You only have I sinned
And done what is evil in Your sight."
And then help me to rest
In Your mercy
In Your tender mercy
In Your faithful love,
Even as the war goes on.

Take a Moment

1. Where does the little kingdom of self tend to get in the way of the work of God's kingdom in your life? (See Matthew 6:19–34.)

2. What thing in life do you tend to want so badly that it tends to control you more than God's call, God's grace, God's glory, and God's kingdom?

19 | The Lord's Prayer

Against you, you only have I sinned and done what is evil in your sight.

PSALM 51:4

I don't think you could say more dangerous words than those found in the Lord's Prayer. I don't think you could pray a more radical prayer. I don't think you could wish for something that will turn your life more upside down than this. I think that most of the people who say these words would probably hesitate if they really understood what they were saying. I think we would all pause before we repeated this prayer if we clearly understood that we were actually praying upheaval into our lives. This is simply a prayer that can't be answered without the tearing down and rebuilding of many things in our lives. Had David prayed and lived this prayer, Psalm 51 wouldn't be in the Bible.

Here are the radical words I have been alluding to: "Your kingdom come, your will be done, on earth as it is in heaven" (Matthew 6:10). I must admit that I don't always greet God's kingdom with delight. There are things that I want in my life, and I not only want them, but I know how, when, and where I want them! I want my life to be comfortable. I want my schedule to be unobstructed and predictable. I want the people around me to esteem and appreciate me. I want control over the situations and relationships in my life. I want people to affirm my opinions and follow my lead. I want the pleasures that I find entertaining to be available to me. I want the ministry initiatives I direct to be well received and successful. I want my children to appreciate that they have been blessed with me as their father. I want my wife to be a joyful and committed supporter of my dreams. I don't want to suffer. I don't want to live without. I don't want to have to deal with personal defeat or ministry failure. What I am saying is that I want *my* kingdom to come and *my* will to be done.

In this way I stand with David. In David's kingdom, Bathsheba would be his wife. In David's kingdom, Bathsheba would have had no husband. In David's kingdom he could have Bathsheba and the blessing of the Lord on his reign at the same time. So, David acted out of zeal for *his* own kingdom, forgetting that he was sent as the ambassador of a greater King. Sadly, I do the very same thing. I get mad at one of my children, not because they broke God's law but because they broke mine. I get impatient with my wife because she is delaying the realization of the purposes of my kingdom of one. Or I get discouraged with God because he brings the very uncomfortable things into my life that I work so hard to avoid.

"Thy kingdom come" is a dangerous prayer, for it means the death of your own sovereignty. It means your life will be shaped by the will of another. It means that you will experience the messiness, discomfort, and difficulty of God's refining grace. It means surrendering the center of your universe to the One who alone deserves to be there. It means loving God above all else and your neighbor as yourself. It means experiencing the freedom that can only be found when God breaks your bondage to you! It means finally living for the one glory that is truly glorious, the glory of God.

You see, the prayer that Christ taught us to pray is the antidote to sin. Since sin starts with the heart, it's only when my heart desires God's will more than it desires my will, that I'll live within the moral boundaries that God has set for me. And it is only God's grace that can produce this kind of heart.

"Thy kingdom come," words of surrender, words of protection, and words of grace that can only be prayed by those who've been delivered by the Redeemer from the one kingdom that always leads to destruction and death, the kingdom of self.

Take a Moment

1. Are you willing to say to God, "Lord I commit to doing everything I do, saying everything I say, and choosing everything I choose for the sake of your kingdom and not mine"?

2. Do you find joy and hope in knowing that as God calls you to live for his kingdom he frees you from being in bondage to your own little kingdom of one?

20 | Nathan's Legacy

. . . when Nathan the prophet went to him.

TITLE OF PSALM 51

No shouts
No pointed fingers
No flashing eyes
No red-faced accusations
No inflammatory vocabulary
No bulging forehead veins
No derogatory names
No scary threats
No arrows of guilt
No cornering logic
No "how dare you?"
No "I can't believe you would!"
No "what were you thinking?"
No public confrontation
No published rebuke
No arrest warrant
No handcuffs
No leading away to be charged
No list of crimes
No human tricks
No trying to do God's work
No hope of forcing a turning
No confidence in the power of man
No human manipulation
No political posturing,
No, none of these.
Just a humble prophet
Telling a simple story
A sinner with a sinner
Not standing above

Alongside, together
Wanting to be an instrument
Hoping to assist a blind man to see
But no trust in self
Speaking calmly
Speaking simply
And letting God
Do through a familiar example
Painted with plain words
What only God can do
Crack the hard-shell heart
Of a wayward man
And make it feel again
See again
Cry again
Pray again
Plead again
Hope again
Love again
Commit again
To a new and better way.
Not the legacy of
Self-righteous
Impatient
Condemning
"I'm better than you"
Anger
But the harvest
Of a man of grace
Giving grace
To a man
Who doesn't deserve grace
But won't live again
Without it.

Take a Moment

1. Are there people in your life whom you are tempted to motivate toward change by harsh words, increased volume, tight logic, and angry accusation?

2. In these relationships, what would it look like to function as God's tool of personal insight and change as Nathan did with David?

21 | What in the World Is Hyssop?

Purge me with hyssop, and I shall be clean;
wash me, and I shall be whiter than snow.

PSALM 51:7

It seems such a strange request from a man who's in the throes of grief over sins that he can't deny and can't take back. I would propose to you that it was exactly the right thing for David and for each of us to pray whenever we're confronted with our sins. But when you first read the word in Psalm 51, it does make you wonder, "What in the world is hyssop?"

Researching the plant won't give you much help. It produces a delicate white flower and is thought by some to have medicinal qualities. But this is one time that wikipedia.com won't help you. What you really need to know, in order to understand the grieving in David's request, is Old Testament history. David's mind goes to that original Passover, when the firstborn of Egypt were stricken dead and the houses of Israel that had blood on the door frames were passed over. What does this have to do with David's request? Here it is: God directed the Israelites to take a branch of hyssop and dip it in blood and paint the door frames with it.

Here is David, grieved by his sin and bowed before God between the "already" and the "not yet." Already the blood of the first Passover had protected Israel from death and made their exodus to freedom and the land of promise possible. Already the Mosaic system of constant animal-blood sacrifices covered the sins of God's people. But the promised Lamb had not yet come. Not yet had his blood been spilt, once and for all, in the final moment of sacrifice that forever ended any need for further sacrifice.

So, reflecting on the past, David's words actually reach into the future. They form the ultimate backdrop to the future prayer. For embedded in this cry for cleansing that remembers the spilt blood of deliverance (Passover) and the shed blood of forgiveness (Mosaic sacrifices), David cries for the one thing that anyone who acknowledges his sin will cry for—cleansing.

When your sin really does become ugly to you, when it produces pain in your heart and sickness in your stomach, you celebrate forgiveness, but you want something more. You want to be clean. You long to be once and for all purified from all sin whatsoever. You want your sin to be once and for all washed away. You want to be free of every dark residue of sinful thought, desire, word, or deed.

Yes, you'll love the fact that you can stand before God dirty and unafraid because of his comprehensive and freely given grace. You'll love the fact that his forgiveness of you has been full and complete. But you'll grow tired of needing and seeking forgiveness. You'll mourn the hold that sin has on you. You'll be frustrated with the way that sin seems to infect everything you do. And you'll begin to plead for what the blood of Jesus alone is able to do; wash away your sin. In this moment of need and helplessness, you'll cry, "Purge me with hyssop Lord, dip the branch of your grace into the blood of your Son and cleanse me once and for all!"

David never sang that great, old hymn "Nothing but the Blood," but maybe he'll hear it some day and remember the tear-stained prayer that followed the visit of Nathan. Maybe someday he'll celebrate final cleansing with a chorus of the ages singing:

What can wash away my sin?
Nothing but the blood of Jesus.
What can make me whole again?
Nothing but the blood of Jesus.
O precious is the flow,
That makes me white as snow.
No other fount I know,
Nothing but the blood of Jesus.

Take a Moment

1. Look back on your life. Identify the many, many places where you need to celebrate how God daily delivers you from sin. What things that once plagued and controlled you are no longer part of your life? (Be concrete and specific.)

2. Look ahead. Where do you see the need for more of God's cleansing? What things still tend to tempt and trap you? Pray and seek God's help.

22 | Moral Vulnerability

Create in me a clean heart, O God, and renew
a right spirit within me.

PSALM 51:10

Beauty compelling
Tugging, seducing
Wanting and craving
Weakened resolve;
Lingering, staring
Moral transgression
Look of desire
Selfish rebellion
Act of betrayal
Weakened resolve.
Long consideration
Dreams of possessing
Evil hoping
Enemy lurking
Heart now racing
Battle raging
Nervous thinking
Flesh growing weaker
Drawn to the darkness
Weakened resolve.
Wrong seen as righteous
Plausible lies
Twisted pretenses
Self swindling
Guilty logic
Deluded perspectives
Weakened resolve.
Deciding and choosing
Date and location

Concrete plans
Words of acceptance
Verbal contract
Shared deception
Anticipation
Tracks covered over
Weakened resolve.
Deed now accomplished
Fleeing the scene
Dark of night
Trembling hands
Afraid of discovery
Made up stories
Weakened resolve.
Morning remorse
Hard to imagine
Fear of discovery
Rehearsed denials
Lust unweakening
Purity lost
No undoing
Weakened resolve.
Protecting secrets
Telling lies
Acting the part
Believable excuses
Internal battles
Hunger for more
Weakened resolve.
Haunted by guilt
Crushed by conviction
No more delusion
Power of truth
Weakened resolve.
Stain of iniquity
Remorse of transgression
Cries for forgiveness
Hope for mercy
Cast on compassion
Admission of guilt
Weakened resolve.
Bitter harvest

Sweet forgiveness
The grace of cleansing
Joy in acceptance
Rescuing Savior
Loving Redeemer
Patient Father
Acting in power
Sin's bondage broken
No more compulsion
Freedom is given
Weakened resolve.
Confession of weakness
Tell of His mercy
Worship and service
Willing obedience
Resisting temptation
Steps of protection
Weakened resolve.
Seeking assistance
Sacrifice gladly
Witness to battle
Praise and thanksgiving
Long perseverance
Gone is deception
Weakened resolve.

Take a Moment

1. Try to identify evidence of moral vulnerability in your life. Where are you tempted to see as beautiful what God says is ugly? Where are you tempted to believe plausible lies? Where are you tempted to hide or cover your tracks?

2. Where do you need the help of God's grace so you can confess, seek help, stand and fight, refuse to listen, and speak the truth?

23 | Everyone's a Teacher

Then I will teach transgressors your ways,
and sinners will return to you.

PSALM 51:13

Do you know that God has called you to be a teacher? You say, "Come on, Paul, you've got to be kidding! I've never been to seminary. I freeze up whenever I have to say something in front of a crowd. I don't feel that I'm as biblically literate as I should be. I don't think God really intends me to be one of his instructors."

Let me explain what I'm talking about. It's true that God sets apart certain people for formal teaching ministry in the church. He gives them the gifts and grace necessary to do the thing he's called them to do. But the formal ministry of the Word in the body of Christ is only one aspect of the church's teaching ministry. Paul says, in Colossians 3:16, "Let the word of Christ dwell in you richly, teaching and admonishing one another in all wisdom." It's clear here that he's talking about the myriad of everyday-life ministry opportunities that God will give every one of his children. According to Paul, you have been called to teach. And if you want to understand what that means, you need to understand that there's no real separation between life and ministry. Rather, the Bible teaches that every dimension of human life is, at the very same time, a forum for ministry.

This is where David comes in. He says, in Psalm 51, "Restore to me the joy of your salvation, and uphold me with a willing spirit. Then I will teach transgressors your ways." David is reminding us that what qualifies us to teach in the personal ministry context of daily life is the grace that we have received in our own moments of need. This teaching isn't about laying out a comprehensive theology of grace. Most of us wouldn't be qualified to do that. No, what it's actually about is realizing that my story of God having rescued me by his grace is a tool that God intends to use in the lives of others. As I teach others, by being willing to share my own story, I am actually being a tool of transforming grace in their lives. In this kind of one-on-one, informal ministry, I'm not teaching the person *about* grace. No, I am sharing my *experience* of grace. People learn, not because I've opened the dictionary of grace, but because I've shown them the video of grace in operation.

So, are you a good steward of your story of grace? Have you thought about how to tell your story in a way that puts God and his grace in center stage? Have you looked around and considered who's living with or near you who could benefit from your story of grace? Where have you tended not to let your gratitude shine as brightly as it should? Where have you been unwilling to talk honestly about how much you were (and continue to be) a person in need of rescue?

So, it's true; you have been called to teach. Maybe not as a pastor, small group leader, Sunday school teacher, or foreign missionary. But you have been called to a daily life of gospel transparency, where you're ready, willing, and waiting to share your gratitude for the grace you've been given with someone who needs it just as much as you.

Take a Moment

1. What are your God-given opportunities to teach others God's way?

2. Are there places where God is calling you to teach, but you are remaining silent? Why? Could it be doubt about God, doubt of the truth, fear of man, feelings of inadequacy, busyness, or wrong values?

24 | Natal Trauma

> . . . in sin did my mother conceive me.
>
> PSALM 51:5

You probably don't need me to remind you of this, but there's nothing less innocent than childhood. You see the moral dilemma of children when they are quite young. For example, have you ever seen the body of a yet wordless infant stiffen up in anger? You know the scene. It's nap time. You've fed and changed him. You've sung every song known to human culture and finally he's asleep. You make your way to the door of the room and just as you're ready to make your escape, you hear this ear-piercing scream. You turn around and there he is, red-faced, his entire body rigid with anger. Now you have to visit what's going on there. Clearly, this little one isn't suffering out of need. All of his needs have been taken care of. No, he's angry, and he's angry because at that moment you're not doing what he wants you to do. His rigid-body scream is saying, "Mommy, I love you and I have a wonderful plan for your life!"

Or consider this scenario. You take your five-year-old to Toys R Us. You place him in the cart and you aim the cart down the middle of those wide aisles. You do that because you don't want Johnny to be able to grab everything his heart desires. You get through the store without too much conflict and you find yourself in that final checkout aisle. Now, this aisle is designed to be a conspiracy against your parenting, because at eye level and quite reachable are those $6.95 to $8.95, blister-wrapped items. So Johnny says to you, "Mommy, I want one of those."

You say, "Johnny, Mommy is not going to buy you anything else."

Johnny says, "But Mommy, it's a Captain X Bonco figure, and I don't have any of them. Billy has all of them. He even has the

PlayStation that goes with them. I'm the only boy I know who has to go to someone else's house just to hold a Bonco figure."

You say, "Johnny, I already said that I'm not going to buy you anything else."

Johnny says, "Mommy, if you buy this for me, I'll never ever ask for anything ever again."

You say, "Johnny, you mustn't ask for that Bonco figure again; this puzzle is the only thing I'm going to buy today."

At that point, Johnny begins to scream. It's embarrassing to have this encounter take place as people are waiting behind you to check out.

Let's examine this moment. Johnny doesn't want a mom to provide for him. Johnny doesn't want a God to provide for him. No, Johnny wants to be that God. Johnny wants to think and it will happen, he wants to speak and it will be done, and if you stand in Johnny's way, there will be hell to pay!

You see, when David says, "Surely I was sinful at birth, sinful from the time my mother conceived me" (NIV), he's exposing the ultimate natal trauma. There's a deeper birth trauma than the physical suffering that both mother and child must endure in order for the child to be born. The deeper, more profound trauma is the devastating reality that you can't stop yourself from giving birth to a sinner. It happens 100 percent of the time. It's the natal disease for which there is no inoculation.

But there's more to be said about this universal natal trauma. When David says that he was sinful from birth, he's talking about something more significant than the fact that even babies do bad things. He's actually pointing to why babies do bad things. Being a sinner is about the disease of the heart behind the aberrant behavior. The moral problem of babies is not first about behavior. They have a behavioral problem because they want their own way. They want to live in the center of their own little universe. They want to be the kings and queens of their own little kingdoms. So, they are innately self-focused and rebellious. They have their own agenda, and they don't want to serve the will of another. That's why the infant stiffens his body at nap time and the little boy starts screaming in the checkout aisle of Toys R Us. Both instances of bad behavior are rooted in the most horrible of natal diseases, an idolatrous heart.

This is precisely why David prays for mercy. If my problem is congenital idolatry, then I need something more than systems of behavior modification and emotional management. I need the rescuing mercy of a Redeemer who will take my guilt on himself, who'll take residence inside of me, and who'll continue to persevere until I've been completely cured of the disease that's infected me since birth—sin. Thankfully, that Redeemer has come and his grace is up to the task.

Take a Moment

1. Are you tempted to blame relationships, locations, and situations for the sin with which you actually came into the world?

2. Are you finding hope in the Redeemer who will fight the battle with sin on your behalf until that battle has been fully and completely won?

25 | Wrecking Balls and Restoration

Restore to me the joy of your salvation.

PSALM 51:12

You know whether a house is being restored or condemned by the size of the tools that are out front. If you see a crane and a wrecking ball, the house isn't being restored; it's coming down. Wrecking-ball responses to the sin of another are seldom restorative. This is one of the things that's so striking about Psalm 51 and the history that surrounds it.

If God had had a wrecking-ball response to the sin of David, there would be no Psalm 51. He had every right to condemn David. David was the anointed king of Israel. He had been placed in his position by God in order to be a physical representation of the one true King of Israel, the Lord himself. All that he did was designed to be representative, that is, making the invisible King visible. So, David's position made the horrible sins of adultery and murder doubly reprehensible. It was right for God to be angry. It would have been just and righteous for God to tear down the house of David forever.

But God's response wasn't a wrecking-ball response. No, God's response to David was the small-tool response of restoration. I live in Philadelphia. It's an older city where much old-home restoration goes on. Pretend with me that you wander into one of those grand old stone homes that's being restored. And pretend that we're watching a craftsman remove one of the three pieces of a triple-crown molding that's on the wall of this wonderful old house. The carpenter is motivated by the vision that this house could be restored to its former beauty, so he's not yanking the molding off the wall with a crowbar. He knows that the wood of the molding is dry and brittle and, therefore, susceptible to cracking and breaking. So, he's using the small tools of restoration. He has a lightweight hammer and an

76

apron pocket full of wedges. He tap, tap, taps a wedge into place, then moves a few inches down and repeats the process. Gently, the wedges ease the molding from the wall. You take a glance behind you, and you see three piles that comprise the three types of molding that trimmed the walls. And you're impressed as you look that there's not a crack in a single piece in the three piles.

God's response to the sin of David is the small-wedge response of a Restorer. He uses the small wedge of the sight-giving words of a prophet, who tells a well-crafted story. He uses the small wedge of conviction, causing David's eyes to see and his heart to grieve. He uses the small-wedge of forgiveness, offering David his unfailing love and mercy. He uses the small wedge of reconciliation, drawing David to himself once again.

But here's what's vital for you to understand: he didn't respond in that way just for David's sake, but for you and me as well. Why didn't God have wrecking-ball responses to David's sin? The answer is that God had plans for David and his descendants. God knew that from the family of David would come the Messiah who would be condemned. Jesus would take the full brunt of God's wrecking-ball anger against sin. And he would do that so we would never face condemnation but have the hope of full and final restoration.

So, in his grace God hammers at you, not with the sledgehammers of condemnation but with the small hammers of restoration. He's constantly tapping the wedges of redemption into place. He's constantly working to separate you and me from our sin. He's refinishing us by his grace so that we can shine with his character. We're forever free from the fear of the wrecking balls of condemnation. He was willing to be condemned so that we may live in beauty and for the purpose for which we were first constructed, the praise of his glory.

Take a Moment

1. Where do you see God's small hammers of redemption working restoration and change in your life?

2. Are you thankful for grace that is often painful but clearly accomplishing its work?

26 | When God Is Glad

Let me hear joy and gladness; let the bones
that you have broken rejoice.

PSALM 51:8

In the pain
of my confession
it's hard to recollect
the fleeting pleasures
of my sin.
My shame
hides Your face.
My anguish
drowns out Your voice.
The lingering visions
of what I've done
haunt
my soul
assault
my heart
dominate
my thoughts.
I want to undo
what
I've done.
I want
to turn back time
so that
my thoughts would be
pure
and my hands would be
clean.
But
lust was born

and
the deed was done.
I can't undo
what dark pleasure has wrought.
So I come to You
just as I am.
I bow before You
shamed and unclean.
The searching light
of Your righteousness
puts fear in my heart
and
reveals more stains than
I ever thought I had.
I bow before You
because I've nowhere else
to go.
I confess to You
because I've no other
hope.
There's no place
to run
There's no place
to hide.
I can't escape
what I have done.
I can't erase
my stains.
So in my grief
I ask for one thing.
I long
to hear You sing.
I long
to see You rejoice.
For when my ears are graced
with Your song
and when I am blessed
by Your gladness
and when the angels
celebrate
then I can be sure
that I've been given

the greatest
of gifts
the miracle
of miracles
the thing that only love
could purchase
the blessing that only love
could offer;
forgiveness.

The LORD your God is with you,
    he is mighty to save.
He will take great delight in you,
    he will quiet you with his love,
    he will rejoice over you with singing. (Zephaniah 3:17 NIV)

"I tell you that in the same way there will be more rejoicing in heaven over one sinner who repents than over ninety-nine righteous persons who do not need to repent." (Luke 15:7 NIV)

Take a Moment

1. Do you still celebrate the amazing miracle of daily forgiveness? Is there evidence in the way you live your life that you have lost your sense of wonder at what God has given you?

2. Do you experience joy in things that tend to compete with the joy you have had with the forgiving, empowering, and freeing grace of God?

27 | Sin Is a Relationship

....

Against you, you only, have I sinned.

PSALM 51:4

Sin is much, much more than the violation of a set of rules. Sin is more profound than rebellion against a moral code. Sin is about something deeper than behaving inappropriately. It's deeper than bad actions and wrong words.

As we noted earlier, when you witness the body of an infant, who's not yet able to communicate with words, stiffen up in anger, you know you're dealing with something bigger, deeper, more fundamentally disturbing than a failure to observe a code of conduct. The infant is angry because you're asking him to do what he doesn't want to do. He's outraged that you'd presume to give him directions. He wants to be the king and lawgiver in his own little universe of one. He doesn't want to live under the authority of another. He wants to make up his own rules; rules that would, of course, follow the shape of what he wants, what he feels, and what he determines he needs. The only thing that would actually satisfy him is the one thing that he'll never have—God's position. He was created to live under authority, not to be that authority. So he fights his subjugation in a vain quest for self-sovereignty.

The desire to be God rather than to serve God lies at the bottom of every sin that anyone has ever committed. Sin isn't first rooted in a philosophical debate of the appropriateness or healthiness of a certain ethic. No, sin is rooted in my unwillingness to find joy in living my life under the authority of, and for the glory of, Another. Sin is rooted in my desire to live for me. It's driven by my propensity to indulge my every feeling, satisfy my every desire, and meet my every need.

This is why David says, "Against you, you only, have I sinned." He isn't denying the enormity of his sin against Bathsheba, his viola-

81

tion of his calling to the citizens of Israel, or his capital crimes against Uriah, Bathsheba's husband. What he's understanding in his confession is that every sin is against God. In his conviction, David understands that sin is an act of relationship or, better stated, a violation of the one relationship that's to be the shaping factor of everything I do or say. Every sin is vertical, no matter how thunderous the horizontal implications of it are. It's God, for whom and through whom we were created to live, whose boundaries we step over, because we don't love him the way that we should.

Because sin is about the breaking of relationship, restoration of relationship is the only hope for us in our struggle with sin. It's only because God is willing to love us in a way that we refuse to love him that we have any hope of defeating sin. It's through the gift of adoption into relationship with him that we find what we need to gain power over sin. And what do we need? A greater love for him than we have for ourselves. His love for us is the only thing that has the power to produce in us that kind of love for him.

Sin is a relationship, and it takes relationship to deliver us from sin. Christ was willing to experience the rejection that our rebellion deserves so that we could have the relationship with God that's our only hope as we grapple with the selfishness of sin.

Take a Moment

1. Think about a place in your life where you tend to want to be God rather than wanting to serve God. What would change in your decisions, words, and actions if you intentionally sought to please God in this situation?

2. Where do you practically need the grace of God to say no to the temptation to step over God's boundaries?

28 | The Holy of Holies

Behold, you delight in truth in the inward
being.

PSALM 51:6

In the holy of holies,
Where my deepest thought dwells.
In the secret place,
Of the heart,
Where no one sees,
And no one knows.
In that place where worship,
Sets the course,
For all I say,
And all I do.
In the holy of holies
Where thoughts,
Afraid to be verbal,
And desires,
Never quite spoken
Determine,
What I will seek,
And say,
And do.
In the holy of holies,
Where greed lurks dark,
And anger stands dangerous.
In the shadows,
Where lust captivates,
And envy enslaves.
In that sacred place,
Of the heart,
Where I plan what I will do,
And rehearse what I will say.

In the holy of holies,
Where love is born,
Or succumbs to hate.
Where gentleness,
Falls to vengeance.
In that place where,
Thinking never ends,
And interpretations,
Become a way of seeing.
In the holy of holies,
Where feelings grow in power,
And overwhelm,
What is sensible,
Good,
And true.
In the holy of holies,
Where I stand naked,
All covering gone,
Before You,
What I am,
As I am,
Void of defense,
Stripped of excuse.
Nowhere to hide,
No reputation to polish.
In the place where You,
Can see,
And hear,
And know.
May you do there,
What I cannot do.
May you create there,
What only mercy can give.
May you hold back,
What I deserve,
And give what,
I could never earn.
May you create in me,
A clean heart.

Take a Moment

1. If you had to identify the deepest, most captivating love of your heart, what would it be?

2. Take time to celebrate God's jealous zeal to inhabit the holiest place in your heart without competition or challenge.

29 | The Terrible Trinity

> Blot out my transgressions. Wash me thoroughly from my iniquity, and cleanse me from my sin!
>
> PSALM 51:1–2

The Bible doesn't pull any punches as it describes the scary reality of sin. You have the powerful words of Genesis 6:5: "The LORD saw how great man's wickedness on the earth had become, and that every inclination of the thoughts of his heart was only evil all the time" (NIV). Every inclination of the thoughts of his heart was only evil all the time! Could there be a more forceful way of characterizing the pervasive influence of sin on everything we do?

Or you have Paul building his case for the sinfulness of everyone, which reaches this crescendo: "All have turned aside; together they have become worthless; no one does good, not even one" (Romans 3:12).

Along with this, the Bible very clearly unpacks the underlying spiritual dynamics of sin. Passages like Luke 6:43–45 and Mark 7:20–23 teach us that sin is first a matter of the heart before it is ever a matter of behavior. Romans 1:25 alerts us to the fact that sin, in its essence, is idolatrous. It is when God is replaced as the ruler of our hearts that we give ourselves to doing what pleases us rather than what pleases him.

Psalm 51 is also one of the definitional passages when it comes to sin. David employs three words for sin that really define the nature of what our struggle with it is all about. The first definitional word he uses is the word *transgression*. To transgress means to acknowledge the boundaries and to step willingly over them. I transgress when I knowingly park in a no-parking zone. I know I'm not supposed to park there, but for the sake of personal convenience, I do so anyway. Often our sin is just like this. We know that God has forbidden what we're about to do, but for personal success, comfort, or pleasure we step over God's prohibition and do exactly what we want to do. When we transgress, we not only rebel against God's authority, but we convince ourselves that we're a better authority with a better system of law than the one God gave us. Propelled by the laws of personal wants, personal feelings, and personal need, we consciously step over God's boundaries and do what we want to do.

But not all of our sin is conscious, high-handed rebellion. So David uses a second word, *iniquity*. Iniquity is best described as moral uncleanness. This word points to the comprehensive nature of the effect of sin on us. Sin is a moral infection that stains everything we desire, think, speak, and do. Sadly, no infant since the fall of the world into sin has been born morally clean. We all entered this world dirty and there's nothing we can do to clean ourselves up. Iniquity is like inadvertently putting a pair of bright red socks into the wash with a load of whites. There'll be nothing that escapes the red stain and remains completely white. In the same way, sin is pervasive. It really does alter everything we do in some way.

But there's a third word that David uses that gets at another aspect of sin's damage. It's the word *sin*. Sin is best defined as falling short of a standard. In our moments of best intention and best effort we still fall short. We're simply unable to reach the level of the standards that God has set for us. Sin has simply removed our ability to keep God's law. So, we fall short of his standard again and again and again. In your thoughts you fall short. In your desires you fall short. In your marriage or family you fall short. In your communication you fall short. At your job you fall short. With your friends you fall short. We simply are not able to meet God's requirements.

This "terrible trinity" of words for sin really does capture with power and clarity the nature of the war that rages inside each one of us. Sometimes I do not do exactly what God requires, but I don't care because I want what I want, and so I step over his wise boundaries. Sometimes I look back on what I've done, having thought that I'd done pretty well, only to see ways in which my words and behavior were once more stained with sin. And over and over again I'm confronted with my weakness and inability. I fall short of God's standard even in moments of good intention.

How can this terrible trinity do anything other than drive us to seek the grace that can only be found in the divine Trinity? In our sin we need a Father who's not satisfied with leaving us in this sad state of affairs but will exercise his sovereign power to set a plan in place that will rescue us from us. In our sin we need a Son who is willing to take our punishment so that we can be forgiven. And in our sin, we need a Spirit who will dwell within us, empowering us to do what we would not otherwise be able to do.

We haven't been left to the ravages of the terrible trinity, because we've been rescued by the love of a better Trinity. Thank you, Sovereign Father, for your gracious plan. Thank you, Sacrificial Son, for standing in our place. Thank you, Holy Spirit, for your empowering presence. In you, triune Lord, we really do find help and hope.

Take a Moment

1. How do the three biblical words for sin—transgression, iniquity, and sin—help you to understand the daily battle in your heart between right and wrong?

2. Remind yourself once more of your inability to defeat sin all by yourself and celebrate the power over sin that is Christ's gift of grace to you.

30 | Longing for Jesus

Deliver me from bloodguiltiness, O God,
O God of my salvation.

PSALM 51:14

It is dramatic anticipation at its finest. It is the best of
foreshadowing. Every line drips with the drama of the necessity of
what's to come. It's one of those moments when it's very clear that the
present makes no sense without the future. If you know your Bible
at all, you can't read Psalm 51 without feeling it. If this psalm has no
future, then its cries are the vain screams of the tormented heart of
a desperate man and little more. David's entire hope in the present
is tied to an event in the future. No future, no hope. Welcome to the
story of redemption.

You see, David's sin, Nathan's confrontation, and the resultant
conviction and confession are a mini-chapter in the grand, origin-to-
destiny story of redemption. David's prayer for forgiveness cries for
more than a God who's willing to forgive. David's plea reaches out
for an actual means of forgiveness. You may say, "There was one.
God had instituted a system of sacrifices for the atonement of sin."
But the sacrificial system clearly was not enough. There was one dead
giveaway: every day the offerings had to be made over and over and
over again. The repetition of the sacrifices was necessary because the
blood of bulls and goats couldn't atone for sin. The whole system of
sacrifice itself looked forward to the offering of the ultimate sacrifice
that would finally and completely satisfy God's holy justice and anger,
resulting in no further need for sacrifice.

David didn't fully understand it, but the cries he prayed and
penned in Psalm 51 were a cry for the final Lamb, the Lord Jesus
Christ. This is the drama of this psalm. In acknowledging the power
and pervasiveness of his sin, David isn't reaching out only for full

and complete forgiveness, but for deliverance as well, the kind of deliverance that can only be found in the spilt blood of the promised Messiah, who would someday hang willingly on the hill of Calvary. Psalm 51 is a hymn of longing. Psalm 51 longs for Jesus.

As David prayed for mercy, unfailing love, and great compassion powerful enough to wash away transgression and create purity of heart, he wasn't praying for a *thing*; no he was praying for a Person. Jesus is the mercy for which David prays. Jesus is the unfailing love that is his hope. Jesus is the compassion for which he cries. Yet, David can pray with confidence because the decision had been made. The end of the story had already been written by a sovereign Savior God. Jesus would come at the precisely planned time. His whole life would march toward that dramatic moment when he would in agony cry out to his Father, "It is finished!" and "Father I have done what you sent me to do. I have offered myself as the final sacrifice. Redemption is accomplished."

Every time you acknowledge your sin, you long for Jesus too. But you're not longing for the final sacrifice, because it's been made. No, you and I long for the final deliverance. We long for that moment when we'll be taken to the place where sin will be no more. We long to see Jesus, to be with him, and to be like him. Isn't it comforting to know that that final deliverance has been written into the story as well? It is our guaranteed future. And so we long with hope.

Take a Moment

1. Do you live with anticipation? Do you approach life with hope because you really do believe that there will be a day when our struggle will be over?

2. Is there any evidence in your life of hopelessness, discouragement, cynicism, or despair? Take time to confess your struggle to believe and bask once again in the reliable promises of your Savior, the Lord Jesus Christ.

31 | Already, Not Yet

Hide your face from my sins, and blot out all
my iniquities.

PSALM 51:9

Psalm 51 lives right in the middle of the "already" and the "not yet." Why is that worth observing? Because that's exactly where you and I live as well. We live right in the middle of God's great redemptive story; that's what the already and the not yet is about. If you're going to live right and well, you need to understand where you're living.

Here's where you and I are in the great story of redemption. Already the "mercy," "steadfast love" (v. 1), and "great compassion" (v. 1 NIV) that David cried out for have been provided for us in Christ. The ultimate sacrifice of forgiveness that David's prayer looked forward to has been provided by the blood of Jesus that was spilt for us on the cross. God harnessed the forces of nature and controlled the detailed events of human history in order to bring his Messiah Son to earth at just the right time and place to provide for you and me the one thing we desperately need and cannot provide for ourselves—forgiveness.

Already the Holy Spirit, for whom David prayed, has been given to you and to me. It's almost beyond the limits of our rationality to consider that that Holy Spirit actually lives inside of us teaching, correcting, convicting, and empowering us every day.

Already, God's great book of wisdom, grace, and warning, the Bible, has been given. When David talks about teaching sinners God's way, he looks forward to the gift of the Word, God's ultimate tool of instruction. We live every day with the Word in our hands, celebrating the wisdom that it gives us that we would have no other way.

So, as we celebrate the already, we need to be very aware of the not yet. This world is still a terribly broken place, not yet restored to what it was created to be. There's never a day when we are not touched with its brokenness in some way.

Sin that has wreaked such havoc on each one of us has not yet been finally and totally defeated. The sin that still remains in us continues to affect everything we desire, think, do, and say. Even in our moments of best intention it's right there with us subverting our desires, capturing our thoughts, and distorting our behavior.

The devil, who is the enemy of all that is good, right, and true, hasn't yet been finally destroyed. He still lurks about with deceit in his eyes, destruction in his hands, and trickery in his heart.

So, we live with celebration and anticipation. We celebrate the amazing gifts of grace that we've already been given, while we anticipate the end of the struggles that will face us until the final chapter of the great story of redemption comes. We do live in the in-between. We do live in the hardships of a world that teeters between the beginning and the end. But we don't need to be discouraged and we don't need to fear, because the end of all those struggles has already been written, and so we're guaranteed that the things that are not yet will someday be.

Take a Moment

1. You and I do live in the middle of the great redemptive story. Where specifically are you finding life in the middle to be hard?

2. Where do you need to reach out for God's help and the help of others as you face the difficulties, suffering, and temptations of this broken world?

32 | Your Ultimate Fear

> Cast me not away from your presence, and
> take not your Holy Spirit from me.
>
> PSALM 51:11

What's the thing that you dread most? What's your biggest fear? What are you convinced you can't live without? What would your biggest personal disaster look like? I got to thinking about the question of my own ultimate fear as I was reading Psalm 51 once again. David prays, "Cast me not away from your presence, and take not your Holy Spirit from me." This should be our greatest fear in all of life, but is it?

She had it all and maybe that's why she was so afraid. She was living in a nicer, larger house than she ever thought would be hers. She had nicer clothes and nicer things than she would ever have imagined. She had the uber-successful husband and three beautiful children. She went to a great church. They had wonderful family vacations. She ate her breakfast, on most spring and summer mornings, on the stone deck overlooking the beautiful valley that opened up beneath the hill on which her house had been built. But morning after morning she'd sit there and worry. She'd worry about her marriage: was it really as solid as she thought it was? She'd worry about their finances: was her husband's job as stable as he said it was? She'd worry about her children: were they doing as well as she thought they were? She'd worry about her health and the health of her husband. She'd even think about the possibility of a natural disaster ravaging their property or an economic disaster destroying their finances.

Something very significant had happened to her, and she didn't even know it. The very things for which she'd been so grateful, the very things that she once thought she didn't deserve, had morphed into things that she was convinced she couldn't live without. What she had once greeted with surprised gratitude were now the sources of major anxiety. The things that had once seemed out of place in her life had become the very things that defined her life. And so she lived with a low-register drone of fear through every day.

But there was something else that had changed. The thing that was meant to define her life, and that once did, no longer defined her. There had been a time when everything in her life was defined and evaluated by her relationship with God. There was a time when she greeted God's grace with a surprised gratefulness. She'd been quite aware of her sin and deeply appreciative of the forgiveness that she'd been given. She'd once carried a lively sense of privilege in having been given an acceptance with God that she could have never earned or deserved. There was a time when she would greet each day wondering what she would have done if God hadn't made himself known to her, hadn't accepted her in his family, and hadn't graced her with his presence.

But now these thoughts were no longer center stage. No longer would she identify herself as a sinner, rescued by grace. No longer did she get her meaning, purpose, and sense of well-being from the Lord. Now she was more concerned about losing her mansion than being cast out of God's house. Now she was more concerned about losing her husband than about God removing his Spirit from her. That once heartfelt and wholesome question, "Where would I be without the Lord?" had been replaced by the question of how she'd cope with the loss of any one item in her personal catalog of material things.

But I didn't think long about David or about my friend, because my mind turned to me. What is the thing in the world for which I'm the most thankful? The loss of what thing do I fear the most? The existence of what in my life gives me meaning, purpose, and that inner sense of well-being?

Take a Moment

1. Be honest: what is it that brings the most fear into your heart?

2. What things in your life are you convinced that you cannot live without? Pray for a heart that is so fully satisfied with God that you are able to be content with what he has placed in your life.

33 | Building the Walls

Do good to Zion in your good pleasure;
build up the walls of Jerusalem.

PSALM 51:18

It's always the fruit of true repentance and it's captured in these words: "Do good to Zion in your good pleasure; build up the walls of Jerusalem." When my heart turns from sin, it turns to concern for what God wants and what others need. In repentance, my heart turns from the love-of-self-driven purposes of my kingdom of one to the transcendent purposes of God. And what is God's purpose? He calls me to love him above all else and to love my neighbor as myself. What does this have to do with praying that God would "build the walls of Jerusalem"? Everything!

David's sin wasn't just a sin of the eyes and the body. No, all the wrong that David did was rooted in the sinful thoughts and desires of his heart. David allowed himself to think things about Bathsheba that he should never have thought, and he allowed himself to crave what didn't belong to him. Then he permitted himself to plan what he should never have planned. With a heart now captured, David committed adultery and murder.

The war of sin is not first a war of the body. The battleground on which the war of sin rages is the heart. There's a war of thought and desire that rages in every situation and relationship of daily life. It's a war between the desires of God and the desires of the sinful nature. So, is true repentance just about letting go of wrong behavior? No; true repentance begins with the heart. In true repentance I confess to my selfishness. I confess that my problem isn't just that I do bad things, but that I do bad things because I'd rather have what I want than what God has willed for me. What does this have to do with building the walls of Jerusalem? Everything!

95

So, it's not only that the battle of sin is a matter of the heart; because it's a battle of the heart, all sin is against God. Sin is rooted in worshiping the creation more than I worship the Creator. Sin is about loving myself more than I love God. Sin is about desiring to be sovereign and constructing my own kingdom rather than finding joy in the greater purposes of the kingdom of God. Sin is about forgetting God and living as if I were at the center of the universe. In my sin I exchange God's holy will for my selfish desire.

But because I've replaced God's will for what I want, in my sin I not only don't love God, I don't love my neighbor either. David didn't love Bathsheba; he wanted to possess her. His lack of love is powerfully portrayed in the fact that he murdered her husband! The very fact that sin is about self-focus and self-love guarantees the fact that I'll not love you the way that I should. Here's the principle: if you and I are ever going to keep the second great commandment, we must first keep the first great commandment. It's only when I love God above all else that I'm free then to love my neighbor as myself. Now, what does this have to do with building the walls of Jerusalem? Everything! Let me explain.

Having confessed his sin and having rested in God's forgiveness, David's heart now turns toward the Lord and toward his neighbor. Jerusalem was the epicenter of the national and spiritual life of the people of God. It was the City of God, the place where the great temple of Solomon would be built. For Zion (Jerusalem) to prosper meant that God's blessings of grace were on his people. You see, in this prayer, David is no longer thinking of himself. No, he's praying that the riches of God's grace would be on the lives of all those around him.

But there's more. When he asks for the walls to be built, it's very clear that David is praying for the building of the temple in Jerusalem. You know that because he says (in v. 19), "Then you will delight in right sacrifices." Rather than his mind being dominated by his own purposes, his heart now goes to the purposes of God's kingdom. He's praying that God would receive the worship he deserves and the glory that's due his name. No longer is David's vision dominated by a woman he wants. No, now he finds joy in envisioning hundreds and thousands of people making their pilgrimage to Zion to worship the One who alone is worthy of the adoration of their hearts.

Here's real personal transformation: the man once captured by dark and evil lust is now filled with love for others and a deep excitement with the glory of God. Only grace can create such a fundamental transformation.

Take a Moment

1. Where in your life does a desire for what God wants functionally need to replace a desire for what you want?

2. How is God giving you specific opportunities to be part of what he is doing in your family, neighborhood, community, church, and world? How are you responding to God's call?

34 | Enough

A Psalm of David . . . after he had gone in to Bathsheba.

TITLE OF PSALM 51

Enough is the persistent problem this side of eternity. *Enough* is what we seldom seem to get right. *Enough* is what trips us up, again and again. *Enough* is one of our deepest sources of trouble. *Enough* is what we find such difficulty in being satisfied with. Although the definition is different for each of us, the struggle with our *enough* is that it tends to keep expanding. And when it does, we never seem to have enough.

It's the thing that slaps you in the face in Psalm 51. How could what David had been given not be enough? Born into a family of faith, anointed by the great prophet Samuel, chosen to be the king of Israel, set apart to be the father of the Son of David, the Lord Jesus Christ! How could it not be enough?

Through David, the promised Messiah would come and provide salvation for the world. David's anointing was much, much more than a position of leadership in a tiny little Palestinian kingdom. It was much more than the blessing of God's appointment to a certain place and a certain time. No, the reign of David was about a far greater kingdom, the kingdom of God. And, yes, that reign was about more than a place and time. In his anointing, God was connecting David to time and eternity, for the Lord of David is the hope of history, the king of eternity, the one with whom the Israel of God would one day dwell.

So, why was all this not enough for David? It wasn't enough because what started out as God's kingdom morphed into David's kingdom. What was to be driven and shaped by the will of God became controlled by the desires of David. What was to be motivated by spiritual vision got kidnapped by physical sight and sexual craving. The plan of God that was to bring life, sadly became a plan of man stained by lust and death. Having lost the war between the kingdom of God and the kingdom of self, David no longer viewed what God had given him as enough.

But don't be too hard on David. His dilemma is your story too. You get angry in traffic; you get irritated at people; you overeat; you fantasize yourself beyond God's boundaries; you get addicted to power, possessions, and people precisely because, in your sin, you are not satisfied. What God has given you in the awesome gift of his grace in Christ Jesus is simply not enough. Christ-satisfied hearts live joyfully inside of God's will, while dissatisfied hearts fall prey to all kinds of temptations. Enough is the war that rages inside us every day.

There will be a day when we will be satisfied. There will be a time when what God has given us will be enough. There will be a moment when we will all be so satiated by the presence and glory of the Lord that we will finally be free from the desire for more.

May each day be a step toward satisfaction. May we grow daily in the experience of being filled and satisfied by him. As the old Christian chorus says, "May the things of earth grow strangely dim in the light of His glory and grace." May we say with joy and integrity of heart, "He is enough."

Take a Moment

1. How skilled are you at telling yourself again and again that what God has given you in himself is enough?

2. Where do you regularly tend to struggle with dissatisfaction and discontentment?

35 | What Does It Have to Do with Me?

Create in me a clean heart, O God, and renew
a right spirit within me.

PSALM 51:10

So what does it have to do with me, this poverty child? What does it have to do with me, this homeless birth in a busy town? What does it have to do with me, these shepherds searching for angel-announced hope? What does it have to do with me, this little boy wandering among the shavings of newly planed wood? What does it have to do with me, these dirty feet from dusty paths of Middle Eastern villages? What does it have to do with me, this unremarkable vagabond? What does it have to do with me, this traveler with his motley pack of men? What does it have to do with me, these weird sayings and mysterious stories? What does it have to do with me, this healer man with crowds of broken citizens? What does it have to do with me, these jealous leaders plotting evil? What does it have to do with me, confusing predictions about a future unclear? What does it have to do with me, these hungry crowds fed by a little boy's lunch? What does it have to do with me, prostitutes and drunkards made to feel welcome? What does it have to do with me, these courageous declarations while standing in the synagogue? What does it have to do with me, this palm branch carpet processional? What does it have to do with me, this private dinner in a rented room? What does it have to do with me, this basin unused with proud men at the table? What does it have to do with me, this dark garden echoing with painful prayer? What does it have to do with me, these three asleep, with a friend in torment? What does it have to do with me, this kiss of death with soldiers as witnesses? What does it have to do with me, these trumped-up charges by jealous men? What does it have to do with me, this bruised and bloody back? What does it have to do with me, this crown of thorns with flowers removed? What does it have to do with me, this Roman ruler washing his hands? What does it have to do with me, this cross dragged outside of the city? What does it have to do with me, this dirty, bloody man nailed to a tree? What does it have to do with me, these criminal companions hung on either side? What does it have to do with me, soldiers gambling for the clothes of the accused? What does it have to do with me, sword to the side to finish him off? What does it have to do with me, this scarred corpse placed in a borrowed crypt? What does it have to do with me, these women surprised at the body gone? What does it have to do with me, this story so removed, so long ago? What does it have to do with me, this one wise and suffering man? What does it have to do with me, Palestine graced, hope rejected? What does it have to do with me? This story is my story, each chapter is for me. This unattractive man of humble beginning and ignominious end is the Hope of the Universe. Mercy is what it has to do with me; it is what the sin struggle of my heart, like the heart of David, requires.

Take a Moment

1. If you saw the story of your life embedded in the big story of the Bible, what difference would it make in the way you think about and respond to life?

2. Stop and meditate on the amazing mercy that is now yours because Jesus was willing to come to earth, live, suffer, and die on your behalf.

36 | Immanuel

> Cast me not away from your presence.
>
> PSALM 51:11

You haven't really understood Psalm 51 until you have realized that every word of this penitential psalm cries for Jesus. Every promise embedded in this psalm looks for fulfillment in Jesus. Every need of Psalm 51 reaches out for help in Jesus. Every commitment of Psalm 51 honors Jesus. The sin that's at the heart of this psalm will only ever find its cure in the grace of Jesus.

Yes, Psalm 51 is a prayer of confession. And it's true that Psalm 51 is all about what true repentance produces in the heart and life of a man. Psalm 51 defines how true repentance always produces heartfelt worship. But more than anything else, Psalm 51 is Immanuel's hymn. The forgiveness of Psalm 51 rests on the shoulders of the One whose name would be Immanuel. The Jesus who would provide everything that David (and we) need took a glorious name. It is a name whose implications are almost too wonderful to grasp and too lofty to imagine. It's a name that summarizes everything the biblical narrative is about.

Genesis 1 reminds us that people were created for relationship with God. This was to be what separated us from the rest of creation and defined our lives. Genesis 3 chronicles the horror of people stepping out of the fellowship in pursuit of the vaporous hope of autonomy. The covenant promises of the Old Testament are God saying that he'll make a way for that fellowship to be restored. The cloud of glory in the holy place of the temple was a physical manifestation of God's presence with his people. All of these things were steps on a ladder that was leading to Immanuel. The announcement of the angels to those bewildered shepherds was God's announcement that Immanuel had come. The promise of the Spirit, fulfilled in the visible flames of Acts, declares that Immanuel had come to stay. The hope of heaven is understood only when you grasp what it means to dwell in the presence of Immanuel forever. What is all of this about for you today? David's hope is your hope because David's confession is your confession. You will only get what God has given you when you understand that you need much more than a system of answers; what you actually need is a Redeemer. Why? Because only a Redeemer can rescue you from you! And so God didn't simply offer you legal forgiveness. Praise him that he did that. But he offered you something much more profound. He offered you himself. He knew that your need was so great that it wouldn't be enough to simply forgive you. He literally needed to unzip you and get inside you, or you would never be what you were supposed to be and do what you were supposed to do.

And so the whole redemptive story marches toward Immanuel, the Redeemer who would destroy sin's dominion in our hearts by making our hearts the place where he, in his power, wisdom, and glory, would dwell.

So pray Immanuel prayers. Sing Immanuel songs. Exercise Immanuel faith. Live in Immanuel obedience. Be motivated by Immanuel glory. And be glad the hope of hopes has come. Immanuel is with you now and forever!

Take a Moment

1. Do you live—in the hallways, family rooms, bedrooms, and boardrooms of everyday life—aware of the presence of Immanuel? Do you think of yourself as the place where Immanuel lives?

2. Read Galatians 2:20. Reflect on what it means to live believing that Jesus lives inside of you and empowers you to do what God has called you to do where you live every day.

A broken and contrite heart, O God,
you will not despise.

PSALM 51:17

I am too satisfied
with the things I say
the things I do
the attitudes
of heart
that shape my reactions
day
after
day
after day.
I too easily
accept
quick assessments
of my own righteousness
in situations
where I have been
anything but
righteous.
I am too skilled
at mounting
plausible arguments
structured
to make me feel okay
about what I think
what I desire
what I say
what I do.
I am too defensive
when a loved one

makes an attempt
to call me out
and suggest
for a moment
that what I
have decided
said
or done
is less than
godly.
I am too
comfortable
with the state of things
between
You and me
too relaxed
with the nature
of my love for You
too able to
minimize
my need for Your
grace.
In the recesses
of my private
world
there is so much
that is wrong
that I am able
to convince myself
is right.
There are attitudes there
that should not be.
There are words there
that should not be
spoken.
There are thoughts
that do not agree
with Your view
of me
and mine.
There are desires
that take me in a

different direction
than what You have planned
for me.
I make decisions
based more on what
I want
than on what
You will.
So I am hoping
for
wise eyes
that are able
to see through
the cloud of
self-righteousness
and see myself
as I actually
am.
I am praying
for
wise ears
that are able
to hear through
the background noise of
well-used platitudes
and hear myself
with clarity.
And I am longing
for
a humble spirit
that is willing
to
accept and confess
what You reveal
as You break through
my defenses
and show me
to me.
I am hoping
for
a broken heart.

Take a Moment

1. Where in your life are you too easily satisfied? Where have you been content with things that are not yet what they were meant to be?

2. Where specifically is God calling you to spiritual unrest and dissatisfaction? How would this dissatisfaction change the way you live?

38 | Wisdom Is a Person

....

You teach me wisdom in the secret heart.

PSALM 51:6

Sin is all about foolishness. Sinners are fools who are able to convince themselves that they are wise. When I sin I convince myself that my way is better than God's way, that my thoughts are wiser than God's thoughts, that what I desire is better than what God has planned for me. Sin is all about how a fool is able to swindle himself into thinking that what's wrong is actually right.

Think of sin in its original form in that awful moment in the garden. There would have been no disobedience if Adam and Eve had refused to listen to the voice of another counselor. What was this counselor seeking to get them to do? He was enticing them to question, if but for a moment, the wisdom of God. He was enticing them to think that he was wiser than Wisdom himself. And he was tempting them to believe that they could be as wise as God.

Check out what Moses records as being one of the things that attracted Adam and Eve to the forbidden fruit. Here's what's said in Genesis 3:6b: ". . . and that the tree was to be desired to make one wise." Now, this phrase is worth unpacking.

You and I will never understand the full range of the temptation of Adam and Eve, David, or ourselves until we understand the fundamental nature of wisdom. Wisdom, in its purest form, is not an outline; it's not a theology; it's not a book; it's not a system of logic. Wisdom is a Person. You don't get wisdom by experience, research, or logical deduction. You don't get wisdom by education and experimentation. You get wisdom by means of a relationship to the One who is the source of everything that's wise, good, and true. In talking of Christ in Colossians 2:3, Paul says that "all the treasures of wisdom and knowledge" are hidden in Christ.

Adam and Eve had all the wisdom they needed; no, not in their independent ability to figure out themselves and life, but in the relationship they had with Wisdom, a relationship that hadn't yet been tainted by sin. Tragically, they took the bait, turned their back on Wisdom, and received foolishness—the exact opposite of what the snake had promised them. This act of foolishness and disobedience began a storm of foolishness that has flooded humanity ever since.

No longer wise, now born into the world as fools, we all need to be rescued from ourselves. And yet, even though there's empirical evidence that we're fools (debt, addiction, obesity, conflict, anger, fear, discouragement, fear of man), we convince ourselves that we're wise and head confidently down pathways that lead to destruction and death. The way that seems wise to us isn't wise, and the way that is wise looks to us to be the way of the fool.

You can't argue us into wisdom, because every wise thing you would say is filtered through the grid of our own foolishness.

And so we need what David needed. Blinded by his own false wisdom and able to take tragically foolish actions that would forever alter his life, David needed rescue. No, he didn't need rescue from Bathsheba. No, he didn't need rescue from the temptations that accompany positions of power. No, David needed to be rescued from himself. He was held by the hands of his own foolishness. What David needed was Wisdom to come near and break David's hold on David. Like us, David needed the rescue of the Wisdom Redeemer. Then and only then would he be wise. Then and only then would he see, confess, and turn from the foolishness that had so deceived him.

Thankfully, the One who is Wisdom is also a God of grace. He delights in transforming the hearts of fools. He finds joy in gifting us with the wisdom that can only be found when he's in us and we're in him.

Take a Moment

1. How does the way that you think about and approach daily living reveal pockets of functional foolishness that still remain in your heart?

2. Where do you need to be rescued by Wisdom? Where does Wisdom need to teach and enable you to live in a way that is wiser? Consider eating, relationships, decision making, private choices, finances, work, thoughts, daily habits.

39 | The Hardening of the Heart

Uphold me with a willing spirit.

PSALM 51:12

Could there be a scarier spiritual dynamic than the hardening of the heart? Could anything be sadder to watch than a warm and tender man become cold and hard? Could anything be more spiritually dangerous than the capacity of a sinner to grow quite comfortable with doing what would have once assaulted his conscience? What's worse than coming to a place where you actually have the capacity to feel right about what God says is wrong? What could be more threatening than the thought that, as sinners, we have an amazing capacity to deceive ourselves? David's story is a case study of this kind of danger. David prays for a broken heart because, in his confession, he's realized that his heart has become hard.

When you read the story in 2 Samuel 11 and the words of confession in Psalm 51, you can't help but ask, "How did David get from the anointed king of Israel to a murdering adulterer? How could this good man end up in such a bad place? Such is the dangerous deceitfulness of sin and the disaster of the hardening of the heart. Here's the thing we all need to remember: sin isn't an event; no, it's a progressive movement of the heart that results in disobedient behavior.

Let's consider David's story. David inadvertently saw Bathsheba bathing. The fact that he saw her wasn't sin, but what he did with what he saw began the process of sin. It's clear that David wasn't repulsed by the temptation. It's clear that he didn't seek God's help. Why is this clear? Because of what he does next. David sends a servant to try to find out who this woman is. This isn't the action of a man who's running away from temptation. David immediately begins to move toward what he knows is wrong, and so in his heart he would have to be justifying what he was doing. David finds out that this woman he was lusting after was married. But again he doesn't stop; he doesn't run. No, he uses his political power to bring her to the palace. What did David tell himself he was going to do next? How did he justify what he was about to do with a married woman? As you read the story, at each point you want to scream, "David, stop; don't do what you're thinking of doing!" But he doesn't stop. Upon bringing Bathsheba to the palace he has sexual relations with her. As you read the account, you find it hard to believe that this is the same man that Samuel anointed to be king because of the character of his heart. But the plot thickens as Bathsheba becomes pregnant. Once more, instead of the pregnancy awakening David from his self-deception, it becomes the occasion of even deeper and greater sin.

David does his best to use Uriah to cover what he has done. If he can get Uriah to sleep with Bathsheba then perhaps the pregnancy will be attributed to Uriah, and David's sin will be hidden. But Uriah refuses to participate in David's scheme. So what David does next, in lust-driven anger, is hard to imagine, even though by this time you know that sin now has a firm hold on him. David has his soldiers set up Uriah so that he'll die on the battlefield. And then David marries Bathsheba.

It's a tawdry and disgusting story, one you wouldn't read if it were a paperback at your local bookstore. But the story is helpful, for it pictures how sin is a progressive system of sinful desire and self-deception. It stands as a pointed warning to us all.

I know you're like me, and you too would like to tell yourself that you're not like David; but you know you are. Like me, you too get attracted to things that are outside of the boundaries that God has set for you. Like me, you're quite skilled at covering, minimizing, rationalizing, justifying, defending, or otherwise explaining away your sin. Like me, you don't always stop at the first warning that something is wrong. You permit yourself to step even closer to evil, telling yourself that you'll be okay. Like me, you allow yourself to meditate on things you should repudiate. Like me, you participate in the hardening of your own heart even as you tell yourself that you can handle it, that you'll be okay.

The physical acts of sin are not actually where the real action takes place. By this I don't mean that behavioral sin isn't sin. What

I mean is that the real moral war of sin and obedience is fought on the turf of the heart. It's when the battle for the heart is lost that the battle of physical resistance to sin will be lost as well. When the heart becomes hard, the system of internal restraint that keeps one pure ceases to function as it was designed to function, and we say yes to that which God has called us to say no.

But there's hope for us. Jesus came to give sight to blind eyes. He came to release the captives from their prison. He came to give us new hearts. He came to break sin's dominion over us. He came so that we'd have the power to say, "No!" when temptation comes our way. He came so that we could live with open eyes and soft hearts. He came so that we could turn to him in confession and receive his forgiveness, just like David.

Take a Moment

1. Is there a place where you need to experience the heart-softening power of God's grace?

2. Where has your conscience grown hard to something that ought to prick and trouble it? Conversely, is there a place where you have been unwilling to do what God is calling you to do?

40 | The Grace of a Clean Heart

Create in me a clean heart, O God.

PSALM 51:10

Could there be a more fundamental prayer request than this? Could there be anything more essential than this? Could there be any hope more beautiful than to believe that someday your heart and mine will be totally free from impurity of any kind? This is the most radical claim of all the claims of the gospel. This is the epicenter of what the cross of Jesus Christ alone can produce. This is the thing that the keeping of the law could never do. Sin is a tragedy of the heart. Redemption is about the fundamental reorientation and restoration of the heart. That David would pray such a prayer not only tells you much about his own sense of need, but it also tells how great his faith is in the transforming power of the grace of God.

Let's think about the theology of the heart that's behind David's request. Human beings have been made by God in two parts, the inner man and the outer man. The outer man is your physical self, your body. The body is the house you've been given for your heart. It is your "earth suit." Someday you and I will get a new suit. (Some of us are particularly relieved that this is true!) The inner man is given many names: mind, emotion, will, soul, spirit, to name a few. All of these terms are collected into one big basket term, *heart*. The heart is the control center of the human being. It's the center of your emotions, cognition, and desires. The heart is discussed in over nine hundred passages of Scripture. It's one of the Bible's most well-developed themes. Essentially, what the Bible says is that the heart is the steering wheel of the human being. The heart controls, shapes, and directs everything you choose, say, and do. What controls the heart will therefore exercise unavoidable control over your behavior.

What does this have to do with David's courageous request?

David understands something that's fundamental to repentance. It's that sin isn't first a matter of behavior; it's first a matter of the heart. That's why Jesus said that to look at a woman and lust after her carries the moral value of the physical act of adultery. You see, since your heart guides your actions and words, if you allow your heart to lust, it won't be long before you commit the physical act.

Or we could look at the other side of the coin. Worship is not first an activity. No, worship is first a position of the heart. It's only when my heart esteems God above everything else that I'll serve him with my time, energy, money, and strength. Impurity of the heart is not primarily about bad thoughts or bad desires. No, impurity of the heart is really about love for something in the creation replacing love that I was only ever meant to have for the Creator. And when I love something in creation more than I love God, I'll think, desire, say, and do bad things.

Now, what all of this means is that our biggest, most abiding, most life-shaping problem exists inside of us and not outside of us. What we actually need to be rescued from is us. What needs to be transformed in our lives is not so much our situation and relationships (although they need transformation as well). What really needs to be transformed are our hearts. What we need are hearts that are clean, that are single-focused in their allegiance to God and his glory. We need grace to transform what we love, what we crave, and what we serve. And what's the bright and golden promise of the cross of Jesus Christ? It's a new heart!

Here's the gorgeous message of the gospel: even though I've bowed again and again to an endless catalog of God replacements, even though I've loved myself more than I've loved God, even though I've rebelled against God's kingdom and sought to set up my own kingdom, God comes to me in grace and wraps arms of love around me and begins a process that will result in the total transformation of the core of my personhood, the heart. He won't rest and he won't relent until he's created in you and me a completely pure heart!

So we wake up every morning knowing that by his grace our hearts are purer than they once were, and by his grace they'll be purer than they are today. So with thankfulness for the transformation that's already taken place and with the courage of hope of the transformation that's yet to come, we wake up, look to heaven, and say with David, "Create in me a clean heart."

Take a Moment

1. What tends to compete in your heart for the worship (rule, control, allegiance, power, authority) that only God is supposed to have? How does this "God-replacement" tend to influence your choices, words, and actions?

2. Celebrate the reality that your heart is purer than it once was as you pray for a further cleansing from the impurities that are still there.

41 | Righteous Judgment

....

... so that you may be justified in your words
and blameless in your judgment.

PSALM 51:4

What an interesting thing for a man who's confessing sin
to say! Why would David be talking about God's justice? Now, it
makes sense, when you have the sense to confess, to remind God of
his mercy, but to stand before him and remind him of his justice is
another thing all together.

Let me suggest that there are two ways that the justice of God
should comfort us sinners. First, his justice means that his assessment
of us is accurate. It isn't colored or slanted by prejudice or bias of any
kind. It isn't shaped by any kind of hidden personal agenda. God's
assessment isn't weakened by favoritism or the cynicism of previous
experience. God's view of us is pure and accurate in every way. What
he says about us is absolutely true. Every judgment he would make
of wrong attitude, thought, desire, choice, word, or action, is valid
and true.

Unlike my experience in this broken world, I don't have to fear
that God will wrongly associate me with some group, or have his
view of me colored by a grudge, or have his perspective on me colored by irritation or impatience. I can rest assured that God's view
of me is trustworthy in every way. And because God's view of me is
untainted by sin, it's clearly more reliable than any view that I'd have
of myself.

Second, the way that God as Judge responds to me is right and
pure as well. God's discipline of me is without personal bias. It isn't
weakened by anger or impatience. His justice is never distorted
because he's lost his temper or has tired of dealing with me. To add
to this, since he isn't only just, but also merciful, loving, and kind

as well, God's justice is always restrained and tempered by these things. He's a God of mercy who metes out justice. He disciplines us in love. His kindness colors how he responds to the sins of his children. The way that God exercises his power is without blemish. He isn't like the leaders we're used to, who use power for personal control or privilege. He isn't like a leader who has an inner circle of sycophants that he treats differently from everyone else. He doesn't use his power to place people in his debt or to use situations to his advantage. His justice is the benevolent justice of a holy king.

So, I can place myself in the hands of the justice of the one who sees me with accuracy and deals with me righteously. But there's even something more here. Unlike David who looked forward to the coming of his future "son," the Lord Jesus Christ, we look back on the life of that Son lived on our behalf. We stand before God unafraid, not because we're acceptable to him, but because his justice has been satisfied by the death of Jesus. So, God is to us both the One who's just and the One who justifies! He can forgive my rebellion and sin without compromising the purity of his justice in any way.

I don't have to manipulate God's view of me.
I don't have to run from him in fear.
I don't have to rationalize away my wrongs.
I don't have to work to shift the blame to someone else.
I don't have to put forward false pretenses.
I don't have to marshal arguments for my acceptability.
I don't have to try to buy my way into his favor.

No, I can be who I am and what I am and stand in the light of his righteousness without fear, because Jesus has taken my sin and suffered my stripes. So the One who is my Judge is also my Justifier. There is rest. There is hope.

Take a Moment

1. Stop and consider how sweet it is that you stand before a God whose assessment of you is not colored by ugly prejudice or self-serving bias. Think of how comforting it is to know that his view of you is always accurate and true.

2. Celebrate the fact that God's pure justice is tempered by his mercy. Celebrate the reality that even though not one of us is perfect, because of Christ he has accepted us without any compromise of his righteousness. In light of this it is an act of gospel irrationality to hide from him in any way. Is there any evidence of hiding from God in your life?

42 | God's Pleasure

> Then you will delight in right sacrifices,
> in burnt offerings and whole burnt offerings;
> then bulls will be offered on your altar.
>
> PSALM 51:19

I must admit
I am embarrassed
by
what gives me
pleasure.
It doesn't take
much
to make me
smile.
I get
real pleasure
from
a good steak
nice chocolate
a comfortable
bed.
I want the joy
of
cold soda
and
hot tea.
I want the bathroom
to
be empty when
I need it.
I want the streets
I drive on
to

be free of other
drivers.
I want people
to
respect my opinions
and
validate my plans.
I want my wife
to
be satisfied
with me as
I am.
I want
my bills all
paid
and plenty of money
to
do the pleasurable
things
that make me
happy.
But God
isn't like
me.
His pleasures
aren't a sad
catalog
of
low-grade
idolatries.
His desires
aren't shaped
by
ravenous self-focus.
He
doesn't
live
in a perpetual state
of
self-absorbed
discontent.
His pleasures

are never
regrettable
ugly
or
unholy.
When
God smiles
His reason
is holy
and His purpose
is
pure.
He finds
great pleasure
in His glory
and
great joy
when
the repentant
turn
from the pursuit
of
their own glory and
turn
toward His.
He has
great pleasure
in
the success
of
His plan
and finds
satisfaction
in seeing
His children
turn
from their pleasure
to
live for
His.
Someday
by His grace

the pleasures
that give me
pleasure
will be
the things that
please God.
Until then
my
hope is in the
fact
that He finds
delight
in rescuing those
who
have been led
astray
by their pleasures
because
once more today
I'm
going to need
that rescue.
And I'll need
it
every day until
my
deepest pleasures
are nowhere to be found
in
the creation
and only to be found
in
the Creator.

Take a Moment

1. How close is what gives you pleasure to what gives God pleasure?

2. If the glory of God was your highest pleasure, what pleasures would you no longer live in pursuit of?

43 | Sermon on the Mount

Behold, you delight in truth in the inward being,
and you teach me wisdom in the secret heart.

PSALM 51:6

Confession results in deeper personal insight. Further confession leads to greater insight. This is one of the graces of confession. You see this spiritual dynamic operating in the life of David in Psalm 51. This man, who was so completely blinded by his own lust that he wasn't able only to use his God-given position of political power to take another man's wife but also to put a contract out on her husband and have him killed, is now able to see not only his behavioral wrongs but the heart behind them as well.

Whenever anyone is able to see himself with this level of clarity, you know that God's grace is operating in his life.

Hear David's words: "Surely you desire truth in the inner parts; you teach me wisdom in the inmost place" (v. 6 NIV). David is recognizing a new awareness. He is acknowledging a new sightedness. He understands what God is working on.

You and I will only ever be holy by God's definition if we put the moral fences where God puts them. We tend to put the fences at the boundary of behavior. For example, rather than telling our children the importance of a respectful heart and the issues of heart that cause us not to respect others as we should, we instruct our children to use titles of respect when they're relating to others. Now, there's nothing wrong with this as far as it goes; the problem is that enforcing certain behaviors won't create a spirit of respectfulness. A child who's mad at his teacher for an assignment she's given may say, "Whatever you say, Mrs. Smith!" in a tone that's anything but respectful. The teacher immediately knows that the child has used a title of respect to tell her that he doesn't respect her at all, but to tell her that in a way that won't get him into trouble!

This is where Christ's teaching from the Sermon on the Mount is so helpful. Christ draws the fences in much closer. He calls for us to fence our hearts because he knows that it's only when we fence the heart that we'll willingly and successfully stay inside God-appointed behavioral fences. So he says, "You have heard that it was said, 'You shall not commit adultery.' But I say to you that everyone who looks at a woman with lustful intent has already committed adultery with her in his heart" (Matthew 5:27–28).

Consider the importance of what Christ does here. He isn't adding to the seventh commandment. No, he's interpreting it for us. He's telling us what the intention and extent of the command has always been. The commandments all address fundamental issues of the heart, or as David says, "the inmost place." The commandments not only depict God's claim over our behavior, but more fundamentally God's ownership over our hearts. But there's something else of importance here. God knows what lust lusts for. Lust doesn't lust for more lust. Lust lusts for the physical experience of the thing that's the object of the lust. A heart controlled by sexual lust won't be satisfied with better and more graphic fantasies. No, a lustful heart craves the actual experience and will only be satisfied when it has actually experienced the thing for which it lusts. This is why it never works to put the fences at the boundary of behavior. Even if I've placed clear fences there, I'll cut through them or climb over them if I haven't first fenced my heart.

Now, again, David speaks for all of us, and his words are so echoed by Christ that it almost appears as if Christ was thinking of David and Bathsheba when he spoke these words.

Have you fenced your heart? Have you tried to stay inside of behavioral boundaries only to have climbed over them again and again? Go and read the wisdom of the Sermon on the Mount, which is found in Matthew 5 through 7, and ask God to "teach you wisdom in the inmost place." By God's grace, determine to fight the battle of thought and desire, knowing full well that it's only when you win this battle that you can be successful in the battle of behavior. And rest assured that when you fight this battle you aren't fighting alone, but your Lord wages war on your behalf.

Take a Moment

1. What "fences of the heart" do you need to erect that are not there now?

2. Where is there evidence that you are stepping over God's "boundaries of the heart?" Stop and confess and receive God's offer of forgiveness.

44 | Appealing to God's Glory

> Then you will delight in right sacrifices . . . ; then
> bulls will be offered on your altar.
>
> PSALM 51:19

You're always in a safe place when you're appealing to God's glory. This is exactly what David does in Psalm 51:18–19: "In your good pleasure make Zion prosper; build up the walls of Jerusalem" (NIV). Why? "Then there will be righteous sacrifices, whole burnt offerings to delight you; then bulls will be offered on your altar" (NIV). David is essentially saying, "God, bless your people, because if you do, they'll live for your glory." This is what all truly biblical prayer will do. We often reduce prayer to a laundry list of self-focused needs in which we ask God to exercise his power for the sake of our comfort or for the purpose of self-glory. You know the requests:

"God, give me wisdom at work (so I can make more money and acquire more power)."

"God, alleviate my financial woes (so I have more money to spend on the pleasure and possessions that will make me happy)."

"God, help my daughter to be more respectful (so that my evenings will be more peaceful so I can get the things done that I want to get done)."

"God, work in the life of my husband (so I can finally experience the marriage of my dreams)."

"God, give me a better relationship with my neighbor (so he will like me enough to make his dog quit trampling my flower beds)."

"God, please heal my body (so that I can do the physical things that I love to do)."

So much of our prayer has nothing to do with the glory of God. Regrettably, in much of our prayer we're actually asking God to endorse our pursuit of a whole catalog of self-focused false glories.

For God to be willing to do that would not only mean a denial of who he is, but it would also mean our destruction.

But perhaps you're thinking, "Paul, it doesn't seem loving for God to be so focused on his own glory. How does it help me to have God's zeal for his own glory be greater than his zeal for anything else?" This is a very good question and worthy of an answer.

First, don't fall into evaluating the character of God as you'd evaluate the character of a human being. God is not a man and cannot be judged by the standards that he has set for human beings. For a human to be obsessed by his own glory would be a horrendous spirit of pride and self-aggrandizement. But not so with God. He's a being of a different kind. He's in a position unparalleled in the universe. To judge God by the laws he has set for people is like judging a poodle by goldfish standards. They are different kinds of creatures. The goldfish was designed to live under water. If you attempt to apply that standard to your poodle, it will drown quickly!

So, it is right, good, and beneficial for God to find his greatest pleasure in his own glory simply because he is God. It's important for you to understand the logic of what you have just read. If God were to deny his own glory, he would by that act cease to be God. To be God, he must be above and beyond every created thing. Willingness to subjugate himself to anything other than himself would cause him to no longer be Lord over all. God's zeal for his glory really is the hope of the universe. You see, the hope of everything that's been created is that the pure, holy, wise, and good plan of God would finally and ultimately win. This is the only way in which all that's been broken by sin will someday be restored. If God would forsake his glory (and therefore, his glorious purposes), all of his promises would have less value than the paper on which they were printed, and the hopes for salvation of every sinner would be dashed. You see, in delighting in his own glory, calling us to live for his glory, and enabling us to do so, God frees us from our self-destructive addiction to self-glory and the endless catalog of false glories that comes with it.

So, God's unshakable commitment to his own glory is the most loving thing he could ever do for us. It's what redeems us from us and breaks our bondage to all the things in life that we wrongly think will give us life but lead only to emptiness and ultimately death.

So when you pray, appeal to God's glory as David did. When you do this you're not only submitting your heart to God, but you're asking him to love you with the kind of liberating love that only he can give you. Each time you pray this way, you celebrate your freedom as a child of God, and you grow in your ability to recognize the difference between Glory and glory.

Take a Moment

1. What created glories tend to compete with the glory of God for the allegiance of your heart?

2. How much of your prayer is dominated by requests that have to do with *your* vision of glory? What changes in your prayer would take place if your prayer was shaped by an appeal to God's glory?

45 | Sacrifices

The sacrifices of God are a broken spirit;
a broken and contrite heart, O God,
you will not despise.

PSALM 51:17

Perhaps
if I give You
some of my time.
Perhaps
if I give You
some of my strength.
Perhaps
if I give You
some of my things.
Perhaps
if I give You
some of my thoughts.
Perhaps
if I give You
some of my success.
Perhaps
if I give You
some of my relationships.
Surely
these sacrifices
will bring You delight.
Surely
these offerings
will bring You joy.
I'm quite willing
to give a tithe
I'm quite willing
to interrupt

my schedule.
I'm quite willing
to volunteer
to serve.
I'm quite willing
to do
my part.
But I get the sense
that You're not satisfied
with a piece of me.
I get the sense
that momentary giving
momentary service
momentary sacrifice
momentary ministry
the momentary turning
of my heart to You
will not satisfy You.
But I must admit
that I'm afraid
of what You require.
I'm afraid of a
broken spirit.
I'm afraid of a
contrite heart.
I'm afraid to be
crushed by Your grace.
So I try to
distract You
with my service
distract You
with my time
distract You
with my money.
Deep inside
I know what You want.
Deep inside
I'm sure of what You require.
I'm afraid
because I want to hold onto
my heart.
I want

to give it to other things.
I want to
pursue pleasures
outside of You.
I'm afraid
to give You
what would satisfy You.
I'm afraid of a
broken heart.
So I regularly offend You
with empty offerings
and vacuous praise.
Hoping
to my own destruction
that you'll be satisfied.

Take a Moment

1. What sacrifices of heart are you yet unwilling to give?

2. Stop and celebrate how Jesus' willingness to pay the ultimate sacrifice enables our sacrifices to be acceptable to God.

46 | The Amazing Grace of Self-knowledge

> For I know my transgressions.
>
> PSALM 51:3

I have counseled people for many years, and one of the things that has impressed me over and over again is how self-deluded people (including me) can be. It's amazing how hard it is to see ourselves with accuracy. It's been my experience over and over again that we see the other person with a fairly high degree of accuracy but can't seem to see ourselves with the same precision. I have had angry people get quite angry when I've suggested that they are angry! I've had controlling people posit that they think themselves to be quite serving. I've watched vengeful people seem unaware that they lived to settle the score with others. I've worked with men eaten with the cancer of lust who tell me that sex isn't a big struggle for them. I've had bitter wives give me the litany of ways they think that they are loving their husbands. I've counseled a gymnasium full of teenagers who really do think that they are wiser than the surrounding authorities. I've sat with ungracious and legalistic pastors and heard them talk of their allegiance to a theology of grace.

Why are we so deluded? The reasons are many. We make the mistake of comparing ourselves to the diluted standards of the surrounding culture, standards that fall far below God's will for us. We also make the mistake of comparing ourselves to others, always able to find someone who appears to be more sinful than we are. We spend so much time arguing for our righteousness that it leaves little time to reflect on the reality of remaining sin. Add to all of this the basic nature of sin. Sin is deceitful. It hides, it defends itself, it wears masks, it bends its shape into more acceptable forms, it points fingers of blame, and it even questions the goodness of God. Sin always first deceives the person who is sinning the sin.

So, since sin is by its very nature deceitful, we need help in order to see ourselves with accuracy. Another way to say this is that personal spiritual insight is the result of community. We don't get it all by ourselves. We need a ministry of two communities in order to see ourselves with the kind of surgical clarity with which David speaks in this psalm. First, we need community with God. He's the ultimate opener of blind eyes. Through the convicting ministry of the Holy Spirit we begin to see ourselves with accuracy and become willing to own up to what we see. But the Spirit uses instruments, and this is where the second community comes in. God employs people in the task of giving sight to other people. For David, that was the prophet Nathan. With the skill of a seasoned pastor, he got inside of David's defenses and told him a story designed to engage his heart and stimulate his conscience. Through the words of this wise man and through the lens of this simple story, David's heart broke as he saw who he was and what he'd done.

There are a whole lot of people who are blindly stumbling their way through life. But their blindness is made even more powerful and dangerous by the fact that they tend to be blind to their blindness. A physically blind person is never blind to his blindness. He's immediately confronted with the fact that he's unable to see, and he gives himself a whole catalog of ways to live inside the boundaries set by this profound physical deficiency. The scary reality is that one of the things that keeps spiritually blind people blind is that they're not only convinced that they see, but they're also convinced that they see quite well! And so they don't seek help for their blindness. Why seek help for a condition from which you are convinced you don't suffer?

So, whenever you encounter a person who sees him- or herself with precision, clarity, and accuracy, you know for sure that grace has visited that individual. It's only God's grace that can enable blind eyes to see, and it's only God's grace that can produce in us the willingness to accept what we've seen.

From the very first words of Psalm 51, you know you're reading the words of a man of unusual personal insight. From the beginning you know you're listening to a man who's humble and clear. People simply don't talk about themselves with such clear and self-indicting words. And so you know this man's been visited by a God of grace and one of his tools of grace, because sinners simply don't arrive at this kind of clarity alone.

Take a Moment

1. In what ways has God's grace enabled you to know yourself better today than you once did?

2. Where do you still tend to participate in your own blindness? Pray that God, in his love, would continue to open your eyes and give you a willing and humble heart to own what he reveals.

47 | Forgiveness

> Blot out all my iniquities.
>
> PSALM 51:9

If the universe weren't ruled by a God of forgiveness, there would be no Psalm 51. It would be an act of self-destructive irrationality to stand before the One who controls it all and admit that you've willingly rebelled against his commands, but that's exactly what David does. He embraces the two realities that, if understood and acted upon, will fundamentally transform his life. The narrative of redemption, that is, the core content of Scripture, is the story of the interaction of these two themes. They provide the sound and smoke of the drama of life in this fallen world.

These two themes are, in fact, the major themes of every system of philosophy or religion. They come to us in two questions that somehow, someway, everyone asks. What is people's biggest, most abiding problem? (Or, why do people do the things they do?) And, how will this problem ever get solved? (Or, how does lasting change in a person take place?) The thing that separates one worldview from another is that each worldview gives a different answer to each question.

By coming to God with humble words of confession, David demonstrates that he's embraced the unique answers that God in his Word gives to these universally asked questions. What's wrong with people? The Bible is very clear and very simple; the answer is sin. The Bible directs us to look inside of ourselves and not outside. The Bible calls us to admit that we are our greatest problem. And the Bible chronicles how sin within distorts our thoughts, desires, choices, actions, and words. But the Bible does more. It shows us how sin puts us at war with God. It demonstrates to us how sin causes us to want to be self-sovereigns and our own lawgivers. Scripture pictures what happens when we try to set up our own little claustrophobic kingdoms of one, rather than living for the kingdom of God. The Bible requires each of us to accept, at the most practical of levels, that we have profound moral flaws within us that we can do absolutely nothing in ourselves to solve.

But David's words of confession prove that David has embraced something else. He comes because he really does believe that there's hope and help to be found. He knows that admitting sin is not a death sentence. He knows that, although he can't solve his greatest problem, there's a place where the solution can be found. The only hope for sinners is forgiveness. To put it even more forcefully, the only hope for sinners is that the One who's in charge of the universe is a God of forgiveness. The bottom line is this: if God is unwilling to forgive, we are doomed. But he's willing! The story that winds its way across the pages of the Bible is a story of God's active willingness to forgive. He controls the forces of nature and directs human history to bring the universe to the point where the Final Priest—the Sacrificial Lamb, the Messiah, the Lord Jesus Christ—comes to earth, lives a perfect life, and gives himself as a sacrifice for our sins. All of this is done so that our deepest problem, sin, will find its only solution, forgiveness, without God compromising his character, his plan, or his law in any way.

The content of the Bible is the worst of news (you are a sinner) and the best of news (God is willing to forgive). It's only when you're ready to admit the worst that you then open yourself up to what's best. All of this means that you and I don't have to live in denial and avoidance. We don't have to play self-excusing logic games with ourselves. We don't have to give ourselves to systems of penance and self-atonement. We don't have to point the finger of blame at others. We don't have to perform our way into God's favor. No, we can come to him again and again just as we are, flawed, broken, and unclean, and know that he'll never turn away anyone who comes to him and says, "I have sinned; won't you in your grace forgive?"

There's no sin too great, there's no act too heinous, and there's no person beyond hope. The offer is open and free. There's no requirement of age, gender, ethnicity, location, or position. God welcomes you to come. He asks only that you admit your sin and seek what can be found only in him—forgiveness. He is able, he is willing, and with grace that we will maybe never be able to fully grasp, he says, "Come."

Arise, my soul, arise; shake off thy guilty fears;
The bleeding sacrifice in my behalf appears:
Before the throne my surety stands, . . .
My name is written on His hands.

He ever lives above, for me to intercede;
His all redeeming love, His precious blood, to plead:
His blood atoned for all our race, . . .
And sprinkles now the throne of grace.

Five bleeding wounds He bears; received on Calvary;
They pour effectual prayers; they strongly plead for me:
"Forgive him, O forgive," they cry, . . .
"Nor let that ransomed sinner die!"

The Father hears Him pray, His dear anointed One;
He cannot turn away, the presence of His Son;
His Spirit answers to the blood, . . .
And tells me I am born of God.

My God is reconciled; His pardoning voice I hear;
He owns me for His child; I can no longer fear:
With confidence I now draw nigh . . .
And "Father, Abba, Father," cry.

"ARISE, MY SOUL, ARISE,"
CHARLES WESLEY

Take a Moment

1. Is there a place in your life where you still struggle to rest in God's promise of forgiveness?

2. Do you really believe that you can stand before God just as you are and be unafraid? Pray that God would fill you heart with this assurance.

48 | Grace That Hides

Hide your face from my sins.

PSALM 51:9

It seems like the last thing you would want to pray. It seems like it would be the thing that you'd fear the most. Who would want God to "hide his face?" God "shining the light of his face" on us is a picture of acceptance and blessing. The darkest moment of suffering for Christ was when God turned his back on him in those final moments on the cross. In a horrible moment of grief Christ cried out, "My God, My God, why have you forsaken me?" (Matthew 27:46; Mark 15:34). Yet, as David stands before God as a humble repenting man, he does what seems to be unthinkable; he asks God to hide his face. What is it that David is pleading with God to do?

On the other side of lust, adultery, and murder, David is filled with the sense of the enormity of his sin. The weight of what he's carrying isn't just about how he used his God-given position to take a woman who wasn't his and use her for his pleasure. The weight on him wasn't just about how he plotted the death of Uriah, Bathsheba's husband. The weight had to do with his understanding of the extent of his problem with sin. David acknowledges the fact that he came into the world with this profound moral problem (Psalm 51:5). He scans back across his life and can't recognize a point where sin wasn't with him. But there's an even deeper awareness that sits on David's heart like a lead weight. He's come to understand that his sin was directly and personally against God. What he did, he did in the face of God. He rejected God's authority and made himself his own master. He rejected God's wisdom and acted as if he knew better. He rejected God's call and decided to do what pleased him rather than what pleased God. In the middle of the outrageousness of his rebellion, how could David ever stand before a holy God?

This confusing request actually demonstrates that David gets it right. He understands the comprehensiveness and the directness of the rebellion of his sin. He understands that as a sinner he can't stand in the presence of a holy God. What David doesn't understand is that when he prays for God to hide his face, he's praying for the cross. Something needs to come between God's holiness and my sin. Something needs to happen so that sinners, like David, can stand in God's presence and be completely unafraid. David couldn't possibly have known where the story of redemption was going, so he asks the only thing that makes sense to him: "Lord, won't you please hide your face from my sin, because if you don't, I am doomed."

The cross was what David was pleading for. The cross provides our covering. The cross provides our cleansing. The cross makes it possible for God to accept us fully without compromising his holiness. The cross allows us to be accepted, not based on what we've done but based on what Christ has done. The cross allows sinners to be declared righteous! Christ covers us, so that as God looks on us he sees the perfect righteousness of Christ that's been given to our account.

Isn't it amazing that the life, death, and resurrection of Christ mean that sinners no longer have to be afraid of God's face? Christ has answered David's prayer. He took the Father's rejection so that we'd be able to stand in the Father's presence and be unafraid. We don't have to ask God to hide his face, and we don't have to search for ways to hide from God. Jesus has made it possible for sinners to stand before a holy God and rest until the sin inside those sinners is no more.

Take a Moment

1. Reflect on how you have been covered by the righteousness of Christ.

2. Have you embraced the fact that your acceptance with God is not based on your position or performance but on the righteousness of Christ that has been given over to your account?

49 | Broken Bones

....

> Let the bones that you have broken rejoice.
>
> PSALM 51:8

I must admit it; I have a low tolerance for difficulty. I am a project-oriented person, so I tend to have an agenda for every day. I know exactly what I want to accomplish and what a successful day will look like. I don't want to have to deal with interruptions or obstructions. I want the situations, locations, and people around me to willingly participate in my plan. All of this means that it's counterintuitive for me to view difficulty as something beneficial. I've little time and tolerance for "broken bones."

My problem is that my Redeemer is the redeemer of broken bones. Maybe you're thinking, "Paul, what in the world are you talking about?" "Broken bones" is a physical metaphor for the pain of redemption. In case you've noticed, God's work of delivering you from your addiction to self and sin and molding you into his image isn't always a comfortable process. Sometimes, in order to make our crooked hearts straight God has to break some bones. I gotta confess, I don't like broken bones.

I love the way the prophet Amos talks about this (Amos 4). It's a bit of a disconcerting passage until you wrap your brain around what the prophet is saying about why God is doing what he's doing. Listen to the "broken bones" phraseology of this passage:

> "I gave you cleanness of teeth in all your cities,
>   and lack of bread in all your places."
>
> . . . .
>
> "I also withheld rain the from you
>   when there were yet three months to the harvest;
> I would send rain on one city . . .

one field would have rain,
    and the field on which it did not rain would wither;
so two or three cities would wander to another city
    to drink water, and would not be satisfied."
    . . . .

"I struck you with blight and mildew;
    your many gardens and your vineyards,
    your fig trees and your olive trees the locust devoured."
    . . . .

"I sent among you a pestilence after the manner of Egypt;
    I killed your young men with the sword,
and carried away your horses,
    and I made the stench of your camp go up into your nostrils."
    . . . .

"I overthrew some of you, as when God overthrew Sodom and
    Gomorrah,
    and you were as a brand plucked out of the burning."

AMOS 4:6–11

Now, you have to ask, "Why would a God of love do this to the people he says he loves?" Well, there's a phrase that's repeated after every stanza of this scary poem that's the answer to this question. Pay attention to these words: "yet you did not return to me." These acts that seem like the product of vengeful anger are actually acts of redemptive love. You see, in doing these things God is actually fulfilling his covenantal commitment to satisfy the deepest needs of his people. And what is it that they need most? The answer is simple and clear throughout all of Scripture; more than anything else they need him!

But this is exactly where the rub comes in. Although our greatest personal need is to live in a life-shaping relationship with the Lord, as sinners we have hearts that are prone to wander. We very quickly forget him and begin to put some aspect of the creation in his place. We very soon forget that he's to be the center of everything we do, and we put ourselves in the center of our universe. We easily lose sight of the fact that our hearts were made for him, and that deep sense of well-being that all of us seek can only be found in him. We rapidly forget the powerfully addicting dangers of sin and think we can step over God's boundaries without moral cost. So, God in the beauty of his redeeming love will "break our bones." He'll bring us through difficulty, want, suffering, sadness, loss, and grief in order to ensure that we are living in pursuit of the one thing that we desperately need—him.

It's time for us to embrace, teach, and encourage others with the theology of uncomfortable grace. As long as sin still lives inside of us, producing in each of us a propensity to forget and wander, God's grace will come to us in uncomfortable forms. You may be wondering where the grace of God is in your life, when actually you're getting it. But it's not the grace of release or relief; no, you're getting the uncomfortable grace of rescue, relationship, and refinement.

So, if you are God's child, resist the temptation to doubt his goodness in the middle of your stress. It's time for us to stop thinking that our difficulty is a sign of his unfaithfulness and inattention. If you are God's child and you still recognize the battle of sin within, then those difficulties are sure signs of rescuing redemptive love. God isn't withholding his grace from you. No, you're experiencing uncomfortable grace, grace that's willing to break bones in order for your heart to be true. This grace is unwilling to give up. This grace will not turn its back. This grace will not accept the status quo. This grace will not compromise or grow cynical. God hasn't forgotten you. He loves you with real love, and he's giving you real grace. And he'll continue to do so until you're finally free of your propensity to wander away. Now that's real love.

Take a Moment

1. What is God doing in your life right now in order to draw you more closely into a more committed relationship with him?

2. Is there a place where you have been willing to accept a status quo that God would reject?

50 | Ready, Willing, and Waiting

> . . . and uphold me with a willing spirit.
>
> PSALM 51:12

Lord,
I think I can honestly say
I am ready, willing, and waiting.
Ready, willing, and waiting
to see my sin as You see it.
Ready, willing, and waiting
to acknowledge that I am my biggest problem.
Ready, willing, and waiting
to run from wrong.
Ready, willing, and waiting
to seek Your help.
Ready, willing and waiting
for my mind to be clear.
Ready, willing, and waiting
for my heart to be clean.
Ready, willing, and waiting
to acknowledge what You see.
Ready, willing, and waiting
to rest in Your compassion.
Ready, willing, and waiting
to hide in Your unfailing love.
I am ready, willing, and waiting
to be washed by You.
Ready, willing, and waiting
to admit that I acted against You.
Ready, willing, and waiting
to prove that You are right and just.
Ready, willing, and waiting

to confess that my problem is from birth.
Ready, willing, and waiting
to examine within.
I am ready, willing, and waiting
to be whiter than snow.
Ready, willing, and waiting
to hear joy and gladness.
Ready, willing, and waiting
for brokenness to give way to joy.
Ready, willing, and waiting
to have a steadfast heart.
Ready, willing, and waiting
to celebrate Your grace once more.
I am ready, willing, and waiting
to teach others Your ways.
Ready, willing, and waiting
to help them turn back to You.
Ready, willing, and waiting
to have You save me from me.
Ready, willing, and waiting
to sing songs of Your righteousness.
I am ready, willing, and waiting
to declare Your praise.
Ready, willing, and waiting
to bring the sacrifice of a broken heart.
Ready, willing, and waiting
to see Your people prosper.
Ready, willing, and waiting
to see You worshiped as is Your due.
But, I am also
Ready, willing, and waiting
to be protected by Your love.
Ready, willing, and waiting
to be held by Your grace.
Ready, willing, and waiting
to be hidden in Your mercy.
Ready, willing, and waiting
to be defended by Your power.
Because I know
that I won't always be
ready, willing, and waiting.

Take a Moment

1. If someone watched a DVD of your last six weeks, would they conclude that you are a person who is ready, willing, and waiting to have God do exactly what he has promised to do in, with, and through you?

2. Are there any specific places in your life where you are less than willing to answer God's call and to do his will?

51 | Reductionism

You teach me wisdom in the secret heart.

PSALM 51:6

There's loads of knowledge to be found, but wisdom is a rare commodity. Why? Because wisdom is one of sin's first casualties. Sin reduces all of us to fools. You see the empirical evidence of the foolishness of sin on almost every page of Scripture. You see foolishness in full operation in the tragic story of David and Bathsheba. This is why David says, "Surely you desire truth in the inner parts; you teach me wisdom in the inmost place" (v. 6 NIV).

You read the story of David's sin, and you say to yourself, "What was he thinking? Did he really believe that he'd get away with this? Did he completely forget who he was? Did he think that God was going to stand idly by and let this happen?" But David is not some extreme case of foolishness gone wild; you see evidence of the same foolishness in each of our lives daily. The components of the foolishness of sin still corrupt and interrupt our lives again and again. People could say of us again and again, "What was he thinking? What was she thinking?"

What does foolishness look like? Here are four of its most significant aspects.

1) The Foolishness of Self-centeredness

We were created to live for something, someone bigger than ourselves. We were designed to live with, for, and through the Lord. God is meant to be the motivation and hope of everything we do. His pleasure, his honor, and his will are the things for which we are meant to live. But the foolishness of sin really does cause us to reduce our lives to the size and shape of our lives. Our living has no greater purpose

146

than self-satisfaction and self-fulfillment. Does this sound harsh? Well, ask yourself, "Why do I ever get impatient with others?" "Why do I ever say things I shouldn't say?" "Why do I get discouraged with my circumstances?" "Why do I give way to anger or give in to self-pity?" The answer is that, like me, you want your own way, and when things don't go your way or people are in your way, you lash out in anger or you turn inward in discouragement. Our problem isn't just the difficulties of life in this fallen world but the foolishness that we bring to them that causes us to trouble our own trouble.

2) The Foolishness of Self-deception

We're all very good at making ourselves feel good about what God says is bad. We're all very skilled at recasting what we've done so what was wrong doesn't look so wrong to us. I'll tell myself that I didn't really lash out in anger; no, I was speaking as one of God's prophets. I'll tell myself that that second look wasn't lust; I am simply a man who enjoys beauty. I'll tell myself that I'm not craving power; I'm just exercising God-given leadership gifts. Foolishness is able to do something dangerous. It's able to look at wrong and see right. Had David been able to see himself with accuracy and if he'd been able to see his sin for what it really was, it's hard to imagine that he would have continued to travel down that pathway.

3) The Foolishness of Self-sufficiency

We all like to think of ourselves as more independently capable than we actually are. We weren't created to be independent, autonomous, or self-sufficient. We were made to live in a humble, worshipful, and loving dependency upon God and in a loving and humble inter-dependency with others. Our lives were designed to be community projects. Yet, the foolishness of sin tells us that we have all that we need within ourselves. So we settle for relationships that never go beneath the casual. We defend ourselves when the people around us point out a weakness or a wrong. We hold our struggles within, not taking advantage of the resources that God has given us. The lie of the garden was that Adam and Eve could be like God, independent and self-sufficient. We still tend to buy into that lie.

4) The Foolishness of Self-righteousness

Why don't we celebrate grace more? Why aren't we more amazed by the wonderful gifts that are ours as the children of God? Why don't we live with a deep sense of need, coupled with a deep sense of gratitude for how each need has been met by God's grace? Well, the answer is clear. You'll never celebrate grace as much as you should when you think you're more righteous than you actually are. Grace is the plea of sinners. Mercy is the hope of the wicked. Acceptance is the prayer of those who know that they could never do anything to earn it. But the foolishness of sin makes me righteous in my own eyes. When I tell my stories, I become more the hero than I ever was. I look wiser in my narratives than I could have been. In my view of my history, my choices were better than what they actually were. Often it isn't my sin that keeps me from coming to God. No, it's my righteousness that keeps me from him. Sadly, I don't come to him because I don't think I need the grace that can be found only in him. I don't seek the rescue of that grace because I'm right in my own eyes.

Sin really does reduce us all to fools, but happily the story doesn't end there. The One who is the ultimate source of everything that's good, true, trustworthy, right, and wise is also a God of amazing grace. You don't get freed from your foolishness by education or experience. You don't get wisdom by research and analysis. You get wisdom by means of a relationship with the One who is Wisdom. The radical claim of the Bible is that wisdom isn't first a book, or a system, or a set of commands or principles. No, wisdom is a person, and his name is Jesus Christ. When you and I are graced into acceptance with him, we're drawn into a personal relationship with Wisdom, and Wisdom begins a lifelong process of freeing us from the stronghold that the foolishness of sin has on us. We're freer than we were yesterday, but we aren't yet completely free. Imagine, there will be a day when your every thought, desire, choice, action, and word will be fundamentally wise! Because of Wisdom's grace, that day is coming.

It makes such sense that a repentant man (David) would reflect on his need of wisdom. Sin, in reducing us to fools, causes us to do foolish things, even though we think we're wise. And for this we need more than information, education, and experience. We need exactly what we find in Christ—grace. Wisdom is the product of grace; there is simply nowhere else it can be found.

Take a Moment

1. Where do you see the four kinds of foolishness still operating in your life?

2. Stop once more and celebrate the reality that there is hope for you, even though you are still a fool in some ways, because you have been brought in to a personal relationship with the One who is Wisdom.

52 | Celebrating Redemption

> O Lord, open my lips, and my mouth will declare
> your praise.
>
> PSALM 51:15

We should be the most celebratory community on earth. There should be a deep and abiding joy that's the backbeat of everything we do. Each of us should carry around with us a deep sense of privilege for who we've become and what we've been given in Christ. We'll spend eternity celebrating redemption, but there's something wrong if the rehearsal for destiny's celebration isn't beginning now.

It should be in our minds, it should flood our hearts, it should be constantly on our lips: we have been redeemed! Chosen out of the mass of humanity, forgiven by the sacrifice of Jesus, accepted into God's family, the Holy Spirit now living inside of us, God working to empower us against and to deliver us from sin, the great paradigmatic truths of the biblical narrative now open to us, the mutual-ministry fellowship of the body of Christ our regular experience, and a guaranteed future in God's presence and free from sin and struggle. We've been redeemed! The scope and breadth of it boggles the mind. It's almost too much for our hearts to take in. Given what we couldn't deserve—love in the middle of our rebellion—and given acceptance we could never earn. We've been redeemed! We've been redeemed! We've been redeemed!

Unlike the rest of creation, human beings are good at celebration. Last night I sat looking out an eighth-floor window over the Philadelphia Art Museum and watched the annual Fourth of July fireworks display. It was a fittingly celebratory end to a two-week celebration of our nation's birth that Philadelphia calls, "Welcome America." Welcome indeed! Welcome to remember the beginnings of the freedoms you now enjoy. Welcome to remember the patriots who gave their hearts, minds, and lives to secure this freedom. Welcome to walk the streets and enter the buildings where American freedom took its shape. And welcome to days of celebration with others who are reflecting, remembering, and recognizing the freedom that now shapes their daily lives. National freedom is a thing worth celebrating, as is another year of life, or the end of the harvest season, or twenty-five years of successful work. But all of these appropriate celebrations pale in comparison to the meaning and majesty of the reality of redemption that should flood the mind of every believer every day.

Hymn writers get it right as they employ the full elasticity of human language to pen songs of celebration. How about this old gospel hymn?

Redeemed, how I love to proclaim it!
Redeemed by the blood of the Lamb;
Redeemed through His infinite mercy,
His child and forever I am.

Redeemed, redeemed,
Redeemed by the blood of the Lamb;
Redeemed, redeemed,
His child and forever I am.

Redeemed, and so happy in Jesus,
No language my rapture can tell;
I know that the light of His presence
With me doth continually dwell.

I think of my blessed Redeemer,
I think of Him all the day long:
I sing, for I cannot be silent;
His love is the theme of my song.

I know there's a crown that is waiting,
In yonder bright mansion for me,
And soon, with the spirits made perfect,
At home with the Lord I shall be.[1]

---

[1]Fanny Crosby, "Redeemed, How I Love to Proclaim It!"

Or what Christian does not know these celebratory words?

O for a thousand tongues to sing
My great Redeemer's praise,
The glories of my God and King,
The triumphs of His grace!

My gracious Master and my God,
Assist me to proclaim,
To spread through all the earth abroad
The honors of Thy name.

Jesus! the name that charms our fears,
That bids our sorrows cease;
'Tis music in the sinner's ears,
'Tis life, and health, and peace. . . .

He speaks, and, listening to His voice,
New life the dead receive,
The mournful, broken hearts rejoice,
The humble poor believe.

Hear Him, ye deaf; His praise, ye dumb,
Your loosened tongues employ;
Ye blind, behold your Savior come,
And leap, ye lame, for joy. . . .

Glory to God, and praise and love
Be ever, ever given,
By saints below and saints above,
The church in earth and heaven.[2]

Or what about this contemporary song of celebration?

Oh, to see the dawn
Of the darkest day:
Christ on the road to Calvary.
Tried by sinful men,
Torn and beaten, then
Nailed to a cross of wood.

---

[2]Charles Wesley, "O For a Thousand Tongues to Sing"

This, the power of the cross:
Christ became sin for us.
Took the blame, bore the wrath—
We stand forgiven at the cross.

Oh, to see the pain
Written on Your face,
Bearing the awesome weight of sin.
Every bitter thought,
Every evil deed
Crowning Your bloodstained brow.

Now the daylight flees,
Now the ground beneath
Quakes as its Maker bows His head.
Curtain torn in two,
Dead are raised to life;
"Finished!" the victory cry.

Oh, to see my name
Written in the wounds,
For through Your suffering I am free.
Death is crushed to death,
Life is mine to live,
Won through Your selfless love.

This, the power of the cross:
Son of God—slain for us.
What a love! What a cost!
We stand forgiven at the cross.[3]

What will you celebrate today? That raise you have been working toward? That new car you dreamed of for two years? The local team that finally won a championship? An anniversary? A birthday? The first steps of that toddler? The lack of traffic on the way to work? The deli sandwich that was better than ever? The new shoes that you thought you would never find? Your new iPhone? If you're a human being, you're a celebrator. The question is, in all of your celebrations, do you turn again and again to celebrate the most amazing, the most

---

[3]Keith Getty and Stuart Townend, "Oh to See the Dawn" (ThankYou Music, 2005).

magnificent, the most mind-bending thing that a human being could be chosen to experience—redemption?

You have been redeemed! You have been redeemed! You have been redeemed! Now, go out and celebrate.

Take a Moment

1. Take time to slowly and deliberately read (or sing) the words of these hymns of celebration one more time.

2. Reflect on what you celebrated this year, this month, this week, today. Who is at the center of your life of celebration?

Personal Reflections

Personal Reflections

Personal Reflections

Personal Reflections

Personal Reflections

Personal Reflections